miracle
soups

Amanda Cross

TED SMART

First published in Great Britain in 2004 by
Hamlyn, a division of Octopus Publishing Group Ltd
2–4 Heron Quays, London E14 4JP

First published in paperback in 2004

This edition produced for
The Book People Ltd,
Hall Wood Avenue,
Haydock,
St Helens WA11 9UL

Copyright © Octopus Publishing Group Ltd 2004

ISBN 0 600 61049 7

A CIP catalogue record for this book is available
from the British Library

Printed and bound in China

10 9 8 7 6 5 4 3 2 1

Notes

Eggs should be large unless otherwise stated. The
Department of Health advises that eggs should not be
consumed raw. This book contains dishes made with raw
or lightly cooked eggs. It is prudent for vulnerable people
such as pregnant and nursing mothers, invalids, the
elderly, babies and young children to avoid dishes made
with uncooked or lightly cooked eggs.

This book includes dishes made with nuts and nut
derivatives. It is advisable for those with known allergic
reactions to nuts and nut derivatives and those who may
be potentially vulnerable to these allergies, such as
pregnant and nursing mothers, invalids, the elderly, babies
and children to avoid dishes made with nuts and nut oils.
    It is also prudent to check the labels of pre-prepared
ingredients for the possible inclusion of nut derivatives.

Safety note

Miracle Soups should not be considered a replacement for
professional medical treatment; a physician should be
consulted on all matters relating to health. While the advice
and information in this book is believed to be accurate,
neither the author or the publisher can accept any legal
responsibility for any injury or illness sustained while following
the advice in this book.

Contents

Introduction

From sop to soup

Originally considered a food for the poor, soup has evolved into a dish for all occasions – from the hearty rustic concoctions which are a meal in a bowl, to light clear consommés and broths which are the perfect way to start a meal, and even chilled fruit soups for a novel dessert.

The word soup comes from the old French word *sop*. This was essentially a piece of bread placed in the bowl to soak up all the juices. This rather soggy precursor to crisp croûtons and fluffy dumplings has all but disappeared, but soup reigns supreme in kitchens the world over.

Grandmother's kitchen

Many people have fond memories of lovingly prepared broths that grandmothers, mothers and aunts seemed to spend hours making – great pots of heart-warming soup bubbling away on the hob with tempting aromas filling the house. Pea and ham, chicken and barley, the remains of a Sunday lunch combined with the gravy. The soup made from the carcass and trimmings of the Christmas turkey is a particular favourite and can be even better than the traditional meal. My most treasured possession is a 1950s enamel 12-litre (20-pint) soup pot – friends and family jokingly refer to it as my witch's cauldron and, indeed, I am never happier than when performing some sort of alchemy with whatever I can find in the refrigerator.

The ultimate comfort food

Nicknamed 'Jewish Penicillin', the ultimate all-time comfort food and cure-all remedy is chicken soup. With its potent mixture of chicken, onions, garlic and parsley, it surpasses antibiotics every time. Most cultures have their own version and countless generations of mothers have turned to the antiviral, antibacterial and anti-inflammatory properties of chicken soup at the first sign of a cold or infection. A wide selection of soups feature in this book so, whether you fancy a fiery Thai soup with plenty of chilli and lime, the soothing Greek Avgolemono with egg and lemon, or a clear chicken and noodle soup, there will be one for you.

Over half the soups included are vegetarian, ranging from hearty chowders with slowly cooked root vegetables to fresh raw gazpachos throbbing with essential nutrients. Grains and pulses have been combined to provide complete proteins, and spices and herbs have been borrowed from vegetarian kitchens across the world.

The move towards a low-fat diet and the high consumption of junk food full of unhealthy hydrogenated fats has meant that in the Western world many of us are lacking essential fatty acids. One of the best sources is oily fish, and here you will find a varied selection of soups based on both sea and freshwater fish. If you are suffering from mental exhaustion and have been working under pressure, then it is vital to increase your intake of fish to at least 2–3 portions per week. Even though you may not feel like making Bouillabaisse when you get home from work, a simple soup such as Fish Soup with Leek & Spinach will take you just minutes to prepare.

Why make your own?

Making your own soup ensures that you are getting the freshest possible ingredients and avoiding the additives and high-sodium content of many commercially prepared soups.

The most time-consuming part of soup-making is preparing the stocks. Even though there are plenty of good fresh stocks on sale at supermarkets, and organic stock cubes, I like knowing where my ingredients have come from and prefer to make a large batch of stock at a time and freeze some for later use.

Once you have made the stock, the rest is easy. With most of the soups in this book, it is just a case of working out whether you want your soup chunky or smooth, hot or cold. The texture and temperature can be varied according to taste.

Why are soups healthy?

Soups can provide you with all the nutrients you need, if you make them with healthy ingredients. A balanced diet requires the following elements, and all these ingredients can be literally thrown into the pot:

Protein: lean meat, fish, shellfish, eggs and soya products such as tofu, pulses, nuts and seeds.

Carbohydrates: whole grains such as rice, barley, wheat and oats, vegetables and fruit.

Fats: healthy unrefined oils, nuts, seeds and a little butter.

Fibre: fibrous vegetables, whole grains and pulses.

Water: very hard to make a soup without it.

Vitamins and minerals: all the ingredients listed above will provide you with the majority of your daily requirements if you eat a healthy balance.

Phytonutrients: soups are an excellent way of ensuring you are getting some of your five portions of vegetables and fruit per day; your phytonutrient levels will be increased if you opt for some of the raw soups, or add fresh vegetables for the minimum cooking time.

Essential soup-making equipment

Liquidizers/blenders: these will process small batches of soup quickly and efficiently. Be sure to allow the liquid to cool a little before blending, and always check that the lid is firmly in place. There is nothing more messy, and potentially dangerous, than boiling tomato soup flying out of a liquidizer.

Food processors: these have many functions, not only to purée the soup but also to prepare the vegetables.

Hand blenders: these are a brilliant addition to any kitchen. Sometimes called immersion blenders, these versatile tools can be used to blend, whisk, emulsify and purée soups and sauces. You don't have to transfer the contents of a soup to a food processor to purée – all you have to do is to plug

in the hand blender and bring it to the pan. Hand blenders are very easy to use and clean, but do ensure they are unplugged from the power supply before attempting to rinse them.

Potato ricers and mashers: the potato ricer is a tool that has been around for quite some time. Not only is it invaluable for making perfect mashed potatoes, it is ideal when you want to thicken a soup. The potatoes emerge looking like noodles and dissolve very easily in hot soup.

Pots and pans: cheap aluminium pans or any other thin, light pans are a false economy. They conduct the heat badly and you spend more time cleaning the burnt food off the bottom than enjoying your meals. It is better to invest in pots and pans made of stainless steel or heavy-gauge aluminium with non-oxidizing surfaces. The base of the pan should be thick and flat on both the inside and outside for better heat efficiency. Pans with metal handles riveted to each side are preferable as they can be put in the oven, along with a well-fitting lid, so you don't inadvertently lose half your liquid.

Fine sieves and colanders: you will need these to make stocks; an effective way to strain a liquid is to place a fine sieve over an empty pan and place the colander over the sieve. This ensures a clearer stock. Further clarity can be achieved by placing a fine sheet of muslin over the sieve. You can also refine the texture of some soups by pushing them through a fine sieve.

Slotted spoons: when you have made a large quantity of stock or soup and need to strain or blend it, tipping a large pan can be a cumbersome job. Removing the bulk of the solids first with a slotted spoon minimizes the risk of an avalanche of bones or vegetables and splashing liquid.

Sprinkles, drizzles and chunks

You can make your soups more interesting and increase their health-giving properties by adding extra ingredients that will increase texture and flavour.

Sprinkle on . . .
Pumpkin, sunflower and sesame seeds
Fresh alfalfa sprouts
Popcorn
Herbs
Chopped and flaked nuts
Wheatgerm

Drizzle on . . .
Flaxseed oil
Extra virgin olive oil
Pesto
Yogurt
Soured cream

Stir in . . .
Protein whey powder
Spirulina

Drop in . . .
Oven-baked croûtons
Cooked rice, barley, noodles

Nutritional benefits of common foods

VEGETABLES

Alfalfa sprouts
Nutrients: Carotene, chlorophyll, calcium, magnesium, potassium, iron, zinc, vitamins A, B, C, E, K, all amino acids except tryptophan
Benefits: Anti-arthritic, anti-asthmatic, diuretic, anti-ageing. A living biogenic food source

Artichokes
Nutrients: Calcium, magnesium, phosphorus, folic acid, vitamins B3, C, K
Benefits: Diuretic, digestive, detoxifies the liver, lowers cholesterol

Asparagus
Nutrients: Potassium, folic acid, betacarotene, vitamins C, K
Benefits: Mild laxative, stimulates the kidneys, antibacterial

Aubergine
Nutrients: Calcium, folic acid, phosphorus
Benefits: Blood cleanser and thinner, protects arteries

Beetroot
Nutrients: Calcium, magnesium, iron, potassium, folic acid, vitamin C
Benefits: Intestinal cleanser and blood fortifier, eliminates kidney stones, detoxifies the liver

Broad beans
Nutrients: Folate, zinc, vitamin B1
Benefits: High in fibre and energy

Broccoli
Nutrients: Folic acid, vitamins C, B3, B5, betacarotene, calcium, magnesium, phosphorus
Benefits: Anticancer, antioxidant, antibiotic, antiviral, cleanses the liver and intestines

Brussels sprouts
Nutrients: Calcium, magnesium, iron, folic acid, potassium, betacarotene, vitamins B6, C, E
Benefits: Contains a substance called indoles that guards against colon and breast cancer, antioxidant, antibacterial

Cabbage
Nutrients: Calcium, magnesium, potassium, betacarotene, folic acid, vitamins C, E, K
Benefits: Cleanses and detoxifies the colon, supports the immune system, kills bacteria and viruses, antioxidant, relieves gastric ulcers

Carrot
Nutrients: Betacarotene, calcium, potassium, magnesium
Benefits: Detoxifier, supports liver and digestive tract, antibacterial, antiviral

Cauliflower
Nutrients: Calcium, magnesium, folic acid, potassium, betacarotene, boron, vitamin C
Benefits: Blood purifier, supports kidney and bladder function, good for high blood pressure, alleviates constipation, anticancer

Celeriac
Nutrients: Calcium, magnesium, potassium
Benefits: Diuretic, stimulates lymphatic system

Celery
Nutrients: Folic acid, vitamin B3, sodium, potassium
Benefits: Anticancer, lowers blood pressure, helps to eliminate water retention, anti-inflammatory

Chilli peppers
Nutrients: Potassium, vitamins A, C
Benefits: Chillies help fight pain,

temporarily increase the metabolism, ease nasal congestion, discourage blood clots, stimulate the circulation, aid digestion, anti-inflammatory

Corn
Nutrients: Iron, potassium, zinc, vitamin B3
Benefits: Brain food, anticancer, great fibre source

Courgettes
Nutrients: Vitamin C, folate, betacarotene
Benefits: Anticancer, lower cholesterol

Cucumber
Nutrients: Potassium, betacarotene
Benefits: Diuretic, lowers blood pressure, good for kidneys, laxative

Fennel
Nutrients: Calcium, magnesium, sodium, folic acid, potassium, vitamin C, phytoestrogens
Benefits: Relieves intestinal cramps, useful for menopausal women as it rebalances hormones, helps to reduce fat

Garlic
Nutrients: Calcium, potassium, vitamin C, allicin
Benefits: Antibacterial, antiviral, antiseptic, cholesterol lowering, thins blood, supports the immune system

Ginger
Nutrients: Calcium, magnesium, potassium
Benefits: Antispasmodic, alleviates nausea and menstrual cramps, relieves indigestion and flatulence, discourages blood clots, stimulates circulation, may relieve rheumatism

Green beans
Nutrients: Potassium, folate, iron, zinc
Benefits: Reduce risk of heart disease, stabilize blood sugar levels, good source of vitamins, minerals and phytonutrients, help to prevent or combat anaemia

Leeks
Nutrients: Folate, potassium, allylic sulphides
Benefits: Regulate blood presssure, stimulate kidney function and fluid balance

Lettuce
Nutrients: Betacarotene, potassium, folic acid, magnesium
Benefits: Aids digestion, promotes liver health, reduces risk of heart disease, stroke and cataracts, helps to reduce the risk of cancer, helps prevent spina bifida and anaemia, may ease nervous insomnia

Mushrooms
Nutrients: Zinc, calcium, iron, magnesium, folic acid, B vitamins
Benefits: Lower cholesterol, support immune function, shiitake mushrooms in particular are meant to contain powerful anticancer properties

Onions
Nutrients: Quercetin, folic acid, potassium, calcium, betacarotene, magnesium
Benefits: Reduce the risk of heart disease and stroke, anti-inflammatory, anticancer, relieve congestion in the airways

Palm hearts
Nutrients: Betacarotene, vitamin E
Benefits: Antibacterial, great for skin and hormonal health

Parsnips
Nutrients: Folate, potassium, vitamins C, E
Benefits: Good source of dietary fibre, help maintain normal blood pressure, involved in red blood cell production

Peas
Nutrients: Vitamins B1, C, iron, folate
Benefits: Help to steady blood sugar levels, richest food source of vitamin B1, may reduce the risk of heart disease

Peppers
Nutrients: Potassium, betacarotene, folic acid, vitamin C
Benefits: Antibacterial, regulate blood pressure, good for circulation, stimulate gastric juices and peristalsis

Potatoes
Nutrients: Vitamins B, C, potassium, iron, folic acid
Benefits: Antioxidant, cleansing, good source of quick-release energy

Pumpkin
Nutrients: Betacarotene, vitamins C, E, calcium, magnesium, potassium
Benefits: Antioxidant, lowers risk of cancer, heart disease, cataracts and strokes

Spinach
Nutrients: Potassium, folate, iron, vitamins B, C, betacarotene
Benefits: Reduces the risk of cancer, helps to avoid and relieve anaemia, may protect against eye degeneration and heart disease

Sweet potato
Nutrients: Richest low-fat source of vitamin E. Also contains betacarotene, vitamin C, folic acid, calcium, magnesium, potassium
Benefits: Contributes to heart health, a good source of dietary antioxidants, can help to regulate high blood pressure, anti-inflammatory, helps anaemia

Turnip
Nutrients: Calcium, magnesium, folic acid, potassium, vitamin C
Benefits: Detoxifies blood, aids digestion, purifies the body

Watercress
Nutrients: Calcium, magnesium, phosphorus, vitamin C, betacarotene
Benefits: Anticancer, counters anaemia, diuretic, purifies blood, stimulates thyroid function, breaks up kidney stones

HERBS

Basil
Nutrients: Calcium, phosphorus, vitamins A, C, folic acid, potassium, iron
Benefits: Aids digestion, eases nausea and motion sickness due to its antispasmodic properties. Dried basil is also good for the respiratory system, can be used to treat nose and throat infections

Coriander
Nutrients: Vitamin C, potassium
Benefits: Good for the circulatory system, digestive system and the skin, also good for migraine headaches

Parsley

Nutrients: Folate, vitamin C, iron, calcium
Benefits: Provides antioxidant protection, counters anaemia, is a traditional diuretic, may help kidney function and gout, cleanses blood, reduces coagulants in the veins

FRUIT

Apple

Nutrients: Calcium, vitamin C, magnesium, betacarotene, pectin
Benefits: Cleansing food, high fibre, antioxidant, anti-inflammatory, anticancer, reduces blood cholesterol, counters constipation and diarrhoea, helps joint problems, prevents disease

Apricot

Nutrients: Betacarotene, iron, potassium, folic acid, boron, copper, calcium, vitamin C
Benefits: Helps to regulate blood pressure, high in soluble fibre which helps maintain regular bowel function, potent antioxidant

Avocado

Nutrients: Vitamins E, C, B6, potassium, folic acid, iron
Benefits: Reduces cholesterol and atherosclerosis, antioxidant, easy on digestion, balances acid-alkaline content

Banana

Nutrients: Potassium, vitamins B6, C, tryptophan, betacarotene
Benefits: Maintains bowel health, energy-boosting, boosts blood sugar levels, promotes sleep, lowers cholesterol, natural antibiotic

Blueberries

Nutrients: Vitamin C, betacarotene
Benefits: Highest antioxidant ability of all fresh fruit, effective anti-inflammatory, anticoagulant, antibacterial, used to combat diarrhoea and food poisoning, anti-ageing properties

Cranberries

Nutrients: Potassium, betacarotene, vitamin C
Benefits: Reduce bladder infections, help to maintain a healthy heart, anti-inflammatory as they have antifungal and antiviral properties and kill bacteria

Grapefruit

Nutrients: Calcium, magnesium, potassium, vitamin C
Benefits: Contains the flavonoid narigenin, which is thought to reduce the risk of some cancers. Also contains salicylic acid, which helps arthritis, improves blood circulation, lowers cholesterol levels

Lemon & limes

Nutrients: Potassium, vitamin C
Benefits: Lemons help to lower cholesterol levels, anticancer effects because of their limonoid phytochemicals

Mango

Nutrients: Vitamin C, betacarotene
Benefits: Supports kidney function, combats poor digestion, good blood cleanser

Melon

Nutrients: Calcium, potassium, vitamin C, betacarotene
Benefits: Anticoagulant action on the blood, lowers heart disease risk, cleanses and rehydrates due to high water content

Nectarine

Nutrients: Calcium, magnesium, vitamin C, potassium, betacarotene, folic acid, iron
Benefits: Diuretic, laxative, cleansing action on kidneys and bladder

Olives

Nutrients: Calcium, iron, betacarotene
Benefits: Anti-ageing properties, protect against rheumatoid arthritis, linked to a reduced breast cancer risk, increase bile secretion, stimulate peristalsis

Orange

Nutrients: Vitamin C, betacarotene, folic acid, calcium, potassium
Benefits: Contains flavonoids which reduce the risk of some cancers, improves blood circulation, lowers blood cholesterol levels, stimulating, cleansing, an internal antiseptic

Papaya

Nutrients: Vitamin C, betacarotene, calcium, potassium
Benefits: Aids digestion, soothes internal inflammation, antiparasitic, fights cancer, a great detoxifier

Plums & prunes

Nutrients: Iron, potassium, vitamin E
Benefits: High antioxidant ability, good defence against free radicals. Prunes are also known for their laxative effect, good source of fibre, beneficial for the blood, brain and nerves, lower cholesterol

Strawberries

Nutrients: Vitamins C, A, K, betacarotene, folic acid, potassium
Benefits: Raise the antioxidant levels in

the body, contain ellagic acid which appears to inhibit the growth of tumours, a good source of salicylic acid, antiviral, antibacterial

Tomatoes
Nutrients: Calcium, magnesium, phosphorus, betacarotene, folic acid, vitamin C
Benefits: Associated with reduced risk of prostate and breast cancer due to high content of antioxidant lycopene, antiseptic, anti-inflammatory

SPICES

Black pepper
Nutrients: Calcium, magnesium, potassium, manganese, phosphorus
Benefits: Digestive stimulant, antioxidant, antibacterial

Cinnamon
Nutrients: Calcium, iron, potassium
Benefits: Stimulates digestive system, relieves nausea

Horseradish
Nutrients: Vitamin C, potassium
Benefits: Aids digestion by improving the blood flow, helps regulate blood pressure, relieves symptoms of flu, sore throat and bronchitis

Turmeric
Nutrients: Potassium, iron
Benefits: The most important source of the phytochemical curcumin, thought to have anticancer and anti-inflammatory effects, a good digestive stimulant

DAIRY PRODUCE AND SUBSTITUTES

Eggs
Nutrients: Calcium, iron, manganese, zinc, B vitamins, healthy protein
Benefits: Boost immune system, build bones, a good energy food

Soya milk
Nutrients: Plain, unfortified soya milk is an excellent source of high-quality protein, iron, calcium, vitamins D, B12

Benefits: Reduces the risk of heart disease and cancer, lowers cholesterol levels, lessens some of the discomfort of menopausal symptoms

Tofu
Nutrients: Iron, amino acids, potassium, calcium, magnesium, vitamins A, K, phytoestrogens
Benefits: Reduces risk of certain cancers, helps prevent osteoporosis, controls diabetes and symptoms of the menopause

Yogurt
Nutrients: Calcium, vitamin D
Benefits: Soothes intestinal tract, generates good bacteria. Live yogurt contains acidophillus bacteria

POULTRY AND MEAT

Chicken
Nutrients: Vitamins A, B3, B6, K, potassium, magnesium, protein
Benefits: Antiviral, antibiotic, breaks up mucus

Duck
Nutrients: Iron, selenium, zinc, full range of B vitamins
Benefits: Repairs tissues, provides energy, supports the immune system

Lamb
Nutrients: Vitamin B12, iron, zinc, copper, selenium
Benefits: Promotes growth and healing, supports the immune system, contains nutrients essential for formation of red blood cells

FISH AND SHELLFISH

Mackerel
Nutrients: Calcium, selenium, vitamin E, omega-3 fatty acids
Benefits: Essential for cardiovascular health, hormone balancing, strengthens immune system

Mussels
Nutrients: Selenium, vitamin B12, zinc, folate

Benefits: Boost immune system, enhance sexual function, cardiovascular benefits

Oysters
Nutrients: Best natural source of the trace mineral zinc (up to 150 mg per 100 grams), iron, selenium and other trace minerals, vitamins A, D, omega-3 fatty acids DHA and EPA
Benefits: Maintain healthy prostate gland, aid in reproduction and mental function. The fatty acids make a synergistic combination with saturated fatty acids from butter and coconut oil

Prawns
Nutrients: Omega-3 fatty acids, protein, iron, zinc, vitamin E, selenium, B12
Benefits: Support the cardiovascular system, lower triglycerides and fat, boost brain function

Salmon
Nutrients: Omega-3 fatty acids, B vitamins, vitamins A, D, E, selenium, calcium, high biological value protein
Benefits: Reduces risk of heart disease, anti-inflammatory, boosts hormones, good for the skin, supports immune system, bones and teeth

Scallops
Nutrients: Selenium, vitamin B12, magnesium, omega-3 fatty acids
Benefits: Heart health, antioxidant, triglyceride-lowering

Tuna
Nutrients: Selenium, B12, magnesium, omega-3 fatty acids
Benefits: Lowers risk of heart disease, blood clots and LDL bad cholesterol

NUTS AND SEEDS

Almonds
Nutrients: Calcium, magnesium, zinc, phosphorus, potassium, folic acid, vitamins B12, B3, E
Benefits: Help reduce the risk of heart disease, lower blood cholesterol levels, anticancer

Cashews

Nutrients: Iron, magnesium, phosphorus, zinc, selenium. Contain significant amounts of phytochemicals with antioxidant properties that protect against cancer and heart disease
Benefits: Essential for red blood cell function and enzyme activity, promote energy release and bone growth, build bones and teeth, essential to digestion and metabolism, important antioxidant properties, low fat

Chestnuts

Nutrients: Good source of B vitamins, vitamin C
Benefits: High-carbohydrate, low-fat, cholesterol-free food, low in sodium and quite a good source of dietary fibre, good for slimmers and people with heart problems

Coconut

Nutrients: Magnesium, potassium, phosphorus, zinc, folic acid, vitamin C
Benefits: Regulates thyroid function

Flax seeds and flaxseed oil

Nutrients: Omega-3 and omega-6 fatty acids, potassium, magnesium, calcium, iron, vitamins E, B3
Benefits: Anticancer effects, may help manage menopausal symptoms, can prevent and relieve constipation as well as soothe digestion

Peanuts

Nutrients: Potassium, folate
Benefits: Contain the phytochemical resveratrol, which has been linked to a significant decrease in heart disease, anti-cancer effects, can lower cholesterol levels

Pumpkin seeds

Nutrients: Omega-3 fatty acids, zinc, potassium, calcium, iron
Benefits: Support the function of the immune system, assist prostate health, help to lower cholesterol levels

Sunflower seeds

Nutrients: Vitamins A, B, D, E, K, calcium, iron, potassium, phosphorus, zinc, manganese, magnesium, omega-3 and omega-6 fatty acids
Benefits: Very high in vitamin E, which is linked to a reduced risk of heart disease, provide antioxidant defence against cancer and cataracts

Tahini/sesame seeds

Nutrients: Phytic acid, magnesium, calcium
Benefits: Protects against free radicals

PULSES AND GRAINS

Barley

Nutrients: Calcium, iron, magnesium, potassium, phosphorus, zinc, folic acid, B vitamins
Benefits: High-fibre wholegrains are thought to lower oestrogen levels. Barley has five times more fibre than other wholegrains, soluble fibre steadies blood sugar levels, may help to avoid heart disease, heals stomach ulcers

Beans (dried)

Nutrients: Calcium, magnesium, phosphorus, potassium, folic acid, protein
Benefits: Lowers cholesterol, reducing the risk of heart disease. Compounds found in beans (isoflavins, lagnins, phytic acid, sapopin and protease inhibitors) help prevent cells turning cancerous

Chickpeas

Nutrients: Calcium, iron, magnesium, potassium, phosphorus, zinc, betacarotene, folic acid
Benefits: Support kidney function, cleanse the digestive tract, good source of vegetable protein

Lentils

Nutrients: Iron, potassium, folate, zinc, B vitamins
Benefits: Great source of fibre which controls blood sugar levels, lowers cholesterol, lowers risk of heart disease, increases bowel health

Oats

Nutrients: Magnesium, zinc, iron, folic acid, vitamin B5, silicon
Benefits: Help to lower blood cholesterol, anticancer, help stabilize blood sugar levels, good for gluten-free diets, ease constipation

Rice

Nutrients: Calcium, iron, magnesium, potassium, phosphorus, vitamin B3, B5, B6, folic acid
Benefits: A calming food, good energy source, alleviates diarrhoea

Rye

Nutrients: Calcium, iron, magnesium, potassium, zinc, vitamin E
Benefits: Unrefined starchy foods aid disease prevention. High-fibre wholegrains are thought to lower oestrogen levels. Barley and rye have five times more fibre than other wholegrains, the soluble fibre steadies blood sugar levels and may help to avoid heart disease

Wheat

Nutrients: Calcium, iron, magnesium, potassium, phosphorus, zinc, folic acid, manganese, vitamins B5, B6
Benefits: Organic, untreated wholewheat with bran and germ left intact stimulates the liver and eliminates toxins

Ailment chart

Acid stomach
Avoid: Coffee, tea, alcohol, sugar, rich creamy foods, cheese, concentrated fruit juices
Eat more: Wholegrains, fruit and vegetables, ginger, lean meats, soya milk, yogurt
Soups: Thai chicken, Yogurt & cucumber, Spicy Indian broth, Spinach & rice

Allergies
Avoid: Dairy produce, wheat, corn, soya, additives, caffeine, peanuts, yeast, shellfish
NB: You should have a food allergy test to isolate exactly which foods affect you
Eat more: Brown rice, lamb, pears, cabbage, sweet potato
Soups: Cabbage, Chickpea & parsley, Sweet potato, Moroccan harira, Spinach & rice

Anaemia
Avoid: Black tea and coffee, foods with an excessively high fibre content
Eat more: Chicken, venison, almonds, leafy green vegetables, tomatoes
Soups: Almond & broccoli, Minestrone, Moroccan harira, Chilled roasted garlic & toasted almond, Oriental beef & rice noodle, Fresh tomato, Spinach & watercress, Duck & plum

Arthritis – osteoarthritis
Avoid: Potatoes, peppers, aubergines, tomatoes, white flour products, pasta, black tea and coffee, alcohol, fizzy drinks, rhubarb, oranges, eggs, fatty and processed meats
Eat more: Cherries, pineapple, oily fish, sweet potatoes, barley, green vegetables, almonds, cayenne pepper, turmeric
Soups: Thai chicken, Prawn & scallop laksa, Spinach & watercress, Almond & broccoli, Chilled roasted garlic & toasted almond, Seared salmon & wilted spinach, Sweet potato, Chicken & barley, Scallop & broccoli broth

Arthritis – rheumatoid arthritis
Avoid: Excess animal fats, dairy produce, tomatoes, potatoes, aubergines, peppers, oranges, plums, rhubarb, tea, coffee, peanuts, chocolate, spinach, beetroot
Eat more: Pineapple, oily fish, root ginger, turmeric, garlic, soya, avocado, green vegetables
Soups: Chilled avocado & palm heart, Fresh herb broth, Tofu & papaya, Thai chicken, Chicken & barley, Curried parsnip & apple

Asthma
Avoid: Salt, dairy produce, meat, eggs, mass-produced pre-packaged foods, foods such as dried apricots that contain sulphur dioxide
Eat more: Green leafy vegetables, fruit, beans, lentils, garlic, onions, ginger, cabbage, oily fish, rice, milk, seeds, unrefined oils
Soups: French onion, Leek, apple & potato, Spinach & watercress, Carrot & coriander, Hot & sour prawn, Lentil & cumin, Lemon & leek

Bronchitis
Avoid: Sugary foods, concentrated fruit juices, dairy produce, refined carbohydrates
Eat more: Fruit, vegetables, sweet potatoes, garlic, onions, chillies, oily fish
Soups: French onion, Bouillabaisse, Gazpacho, Thai chicken, Celery & horseradish, Haitian chicken & orange consommé

Candida
Avoid: Yeast, mouldy cheese, malt vinegar, tomato ketchup, gravy mixes, soy sauces, mushrooms, alcohol, white flour and sugar, very sweet fruits, peanuts, cows' milk, any of the squash family
Eat more: Fresh fish, shellfish, chicken, tofu, artichokes, asparagus, avocado, broccoli, leeks, lettuce, onion, garlic, tomatoes, watercress, parsnips, spinach
Soups: Asparagus & brown rice, Prawn & scallop laksa, Bouillabaisse, Chamomile, cauliflower & lemon, Almond & broccoli, Fresh broad bean with mint, Parsnip & pumpkin, Yogurt & cucumber, French onion, Artichoke bisque

Cellulite
Avoid: Refined and high-fat food, salt, pre-packaged convenience foods, takeaways, coffee, alcohol
Eat more: Water, beans, fibrous vegetables, lentils, seeds, apples
Soups: Chickpea & parsley, Spinach & watercress, Gazpacho, Fennel & tomato gazpacho, Courgette & yellow pepper, Two pepper duet, Cucumber & melon souper cooler

Cholesterol
Avoid: Saturated fats, pork, beef, sausages, cheese, butter, chicken skin, dairy produce, fried eggs, sugar, coffee
Eat more: Raw carrots, fish, beans, lentils, rice, yogurt, soya, almonds, garlic, onions, green vegetables
Soups: Lentil & cumin, Tofu & papaya, Almond & broccoli, Bouillabaisse, Spinach & watercress, Seared salmon & wilted spinach, Fish with leek & spinach, Chilled roasted garlic & toasted almond, Fresh herb broth, Sicilian tuna, Black bean, Courgette & yellow pepper, Creamy wild mushroom

Colds & flu
Avoid: Sugary foods, refined carbohydrates, alcohol, high-fat foods, caffeine, cheese, chocolate, dairy produce in general
Eat more: Garlic, onions, vegetables, lemons, ginger, fruit
Soups: Hot & sour prawn, Prawn & scallop laksa, Carrot & coriander, Tofu miso, Fresh tomato, Borscht, Spinach & watercress, Lemon & leek, French onion, Chicken & barley, Haitian chicken & orange consommé, Strawberry, Japanese chicken, Crab, asparagus & sweetcorn

Constipation & bloating
Avoid: White flour, convenience foods low in fibre, coffee, alcohol, fizzy drinks, cows' milk, cheese
Eat more: Bran, beans, raw vegetables, live yogurt, water, prunes, pears

15

Soups: Black bean, Gazpacho, Fennel & tomato gazpacho, Spinach & watercress, Cabbage, Chickpea & parsley, Minestrone, Fruitcake, Brussels sprout & chestnut, Curried parsnip & apple, Mushy pea & ham

Eczema
Avoid: Dairy produce, coffee, tea, chocolate, citrus fruits, eggs, wheat, alcohol, tomatoes, peanuts, additive-heavy foods
Eat more: Oily fish, seeds, nuts, unrefined oils, fresh fruit, vegetables especially cabbage, celery, beetroot
Soups: Cabbage, Borscht, Celery & Horseradish, Fresh broad bean with mint, Spinach & watercress, Carrot & coriander, Raw energy

Exhaustion & fatigue
Avoid: Stimulants, coffee, tea, alcohol, saturated fats
Eat more: Alfalfa sprouts, fresh fruit, vegetables – especially green and raw, wholegrains, almonds, unrefined oils, oily fish
Soups: Almond & broccoli, Tofu & papaya, Spinach & watercress, Silken tofu & lettuce, Fennel & tomato gazpacho, Chicken & barley, Chickpea & parsley, Gazpacho, Raw energy

Eye problems
Avoid: Alcohol, coffee, salty foods
Eat more: Water, carotene-rich foods such as carrots, sweet potato, mangoes, green vegetables
Soups: Carrot & coriander, Borscht, Two pepper duet, Mango, lime & ginger, Parsnip & pumpkin, Sweet potato, Spinach & watercress, Chunky veggie chowder

Fluid retention & bloating
Avoid: Salty foods, processed foods, salt, alcohol, caffeinated drinks
Eat more: Fruit and vegetables especially spinach, celery, cabbage and blueberries, turmeric, high-quality protein, water
Soups: Celery & horseradish, Fennel & tomato gazpacho, Blueberry & oat, Spinach & watercress, Cucumber & melon souper cooler, Celeriac, leek & sage, Artichoke bisque, Asparagus & brown rice

Haemorrhoids
Avoid: Refined foods, cheese, caffeine, alcohol, dairy produce, salt
Eat more: Unrefined oils, water, lightly cooked vegetables, avocados, fruit, chicken, tofu, beans, pulses, seeds
Soups: Thai chicken, Chickpea & parsley, Tofu & papaya, Chilled avocado & palm heart, Cabbage, Ratatouille, Minestrone, Curried parsnip & apple

Hangovers
Avoid: Grapefruit, saturated fats, processed foods, coffee
Eat more: Broccoli, artichokes, cauliflower, beetroot, celeriac, fennel, celery, oats, water, olive oil, fruit
Soups: Artichoke Bisque, Borscht, Raw energy, Celeriac, leek & sage, Carrot & coriander, Almond & broccoli, Tofu miso, Fresh tomato, Silken Tofu & lettuce, Mango, lime & ginger

Heart disease
Avoid: Saturated fats, hydrogenated fats, salt, pre-packaged, refined and processed foods, fried foods
Eat more: Oily fish, fresh fruit, vegetables
Soups: Bouillabaisse, Carrot & coriander, Spinach & watercress, Almond & broccoli, Tofu & papaya, Borscht, Thai chicken, Ratatouille, Baba ghanoush

High blood pressure (hypertension)
Avoid: Salt, caffeine, sugar
Eat more: Green vegetables, potatoes, beans, garlic, onions, broccoli, celery, coriander, soya, avocado
Soups: Fresh broad bean with mint, French onion, Leek, apple & potato, Spinach & watercress, Gazpacho, Celery & horseradish

Hyperactivity
Avoid: Additives, caffeinated drinks, artificial sweeteners, sugary foods, refined carbohydrates, any foods that you crave – these could cause the problem
Eat more: Organic food, wholegrains, soya products, nuts, high-quality protein, oily fish, seeds, unrefined oils
Soups: Apple & peanut butter, Tofu & papaya, Seared salmon & wilted spinach, Sicilian tuna, Almond & broccoli, Silken tofu & lettuce, Indonesian chicken & peanut, Chamomile, cauliflower & lemon

Hypoglycaemia
Avoid: Caffeine, chocolate, refined carbohydrates, processed foods, sugar, concentrated fruit juices
Eat more: Fibre-rich foods, whole grains, high-quality protein, fruit, vegetables, seeds, yogurt, herbal teas, water, unrefined oils, nuts
Soups: Raw energy, Chilled roasted garlic & toasted almond, Apple & Peanut butter, Black bean, Baba ghanoush, Chickpea & parsley, Asparagus & brown rice, Earth apple, Chunky veggie chowder, Algerian wheat, Souk, Mangetout, mint & caviar

Insomnia
Avoid: Caffeine, alcohol, red meats, too much protein late at night
Eat more: Carbohydrates, fish, chicken, cottage cheese, beans, lettuce, bananas, avocado, chamomile, porridge
Soups: Silken tofu & lettuce, Leek, apple & potato, Chicken & barley, Earth apple, Algerian wheat, Chamomile, cauliflower & lemon

Irritable bowel syndrome
Avoid: Refined wheat products, dairy produce, eggs, citrus, cheese, beef, any flour-based products
Eat more: Brown rice, potatoes, lean poultry, fish, fruits, vegetables, herbal teas, pears, ginger
Soups: Mussel & coconut, Asparagus & brown rice, Spinach & rice, Earth apple, Irish oyster, Chilled avocado & palm heart

Low blood pressure (hypotension)
Avoid: Caffeine, sugar, chocolate, fizzy drinks, refined and processed foods
Eat more: Quality protein, wholegrains, fruit and vegetables, squeezed juices, avocados, celery, fennel
Soups: Oriental beef & rice noodle, Moroccan harira, Mango, lime & ginger, Summer, Japanese chicken, Chicken, asparagus & tarragon, Chilled avocado & palm heart

Low fertility
Avoid: Tea, coffee, fizzy drinks, alcohol, junk foods, sugar, salt
Eat more: Oily fish, seeds, unrefined oils, lean meat, eggs, apricots, leafy

green vegetables, wholegrains, tofu, fennel, alfalfa, beans, nuts
Soups: Seared salmon & wilted spinach, Chicken & barley, Raw energy, Irish oyster, Armenian, Duck & plum, Fish with leek & spinach, Mushy pea & ham, Tofu & papaya, Souk, Mussel & coconut

Menopause

Avoid: Caffeine, spicy foods, red wine, saturated fats, additives, salt
Eat more: Chickpeas, lentils, beans, seeds, oily fish, barley, broccoli, cauliflower, avocado, cabbage, fennel, beetroot, celery, alfalfa sprouts, tofu
Soups: Cabbage, Almond & broccoli, Bouillabaisse, Chickpea & parsley, Chamomile, cauliflower & lemon, Fresh broad bean with mint, Tofu & papaya, Tofu miso, Lentil & cumin, Fennel & tomato gazpacho

Migraine

Avoid: Cheese, red wine, peanuts, chocolate, wheat, coffee, citrus fruits, refined flour and sugar products, additives, hydrogenated fats. Restrict full-fat dairy produce, red meat, eggs
Eat more: Water, flax seeds, live yogurt, wholegrains, fruit, vegetables, tofu, high-quality protein, oily fish, unrefined oils
Soups: Silken tofu & lettuce, Chamomile, cauliflower & lemon, Tofu & papaya, Asparagus & brown rice, Yellow tomato gazpacho, Yogurt & cucumber, Scallop & broccoli broth, Cucumber & melon

Osteoporosis

Avoid: Fizzy drinks, acid-forming foods such as meat, refined carbohydrates, tea, coffee
Eat more: Leafy green vegetables, high-quality protein, pulses, beans, lentils, seeds, nuts, fish, oats, parsnips, alfalfa, cauliflower, sweet potatoes, berries, broccoli, onions, garlic, almonds, peanuts, apples, peaches
Soups: Spicy Indian broth, Parsnip & pumpkin, Lentil & cumin, Earth apple, Sweet potato, Chilled roasted garlic & toasted almond, Almond & broccoli, Chickpea & parsley, Raw energy, French onion, Apple & peanut butter, Blueberry & oat, Chamomile, cauliflower & lemon, Mangetout, mint & caviar

Pre-menstrual tension

Avoid: Animal fats, salt, processed foods, alcohol, coffee, caffeine in any form, sugary foods
Eat more: Water, chamomile tea, high-quality protein, cauliflower, sweet potatoes, broccoli, Brussels sprouts, tofu, soya, seeds, pulses, unrefined oils, lentils
Soups: Chamomile, cauliflower & lemon, Sweet potato, Brussels sprout & chestnut, Almond & broccoli, Tofu & papaya, Armenian, Japanese chicken

Seasonal affective disorder

Avoid: Sugary foods and drinks, caffeine, alcohol
Eat more: Fish, chicken, beans, avocados, wheatgerm, bananas, flax seeds, tofu, beans, green and root vegetables, brown rice
Soups: Seared salmon & wilted spinach, Summer, Black bean, Chilled avocado & palm heart, Chunky veggie chowder, Tofu & papaya, Asparagus & brown rice, Chicken & barley, Chicken, asparagus & tarragon, Indonesian chicken & peanut, Haitian chicken & orange consommé

Sinusitis

Avoid: Sugar in any form, cheese, chocolate, refined carbohydrates, full-fat milk, dairy produce
Eat more: Vegetables, lentils, chicken, brown rice, garlic, onions, ginger, water, chillies and hot spices
Soups: Raw energy, Thai chicken, Hot & sour prawn, Prawn & scallop laksa, Celery & horseradish, Haitian chicken & orange consommé, Lentil & cumin

Stress

Avoid: Alcohol, caffeine, sugar, artificial sweeteners, red meat, processed and refined foods
Eat more: Oats, cooked fruit, wholegrains, avocados, bananas, potatoes, ginger, yogurt, leafy green vegetables, lettuce, oily fish, unrefined oils
Soups: Raw energy, Fruitcake, Chilled avocado & palm heart, Earth apple, Spinach & watercress, Asparagus & brown rice, Fennel & tomato gazpacho, Blueberry & oat

Weight gain

Avoid: Junk and processed foods, refined carbohydrates, artificial sweeteners, salty foods, saturated fats, chocolate, full-fat cheese, too many dairy products
Eat more: Soya milk, whole grains, lentils, chickpeas, fresh fruit and vegetables, cabbage, broccoli, Brussels sprouts, cauliflower, spinach, fennel, celery, apples, unrefined oils, herbal tea, water, flax seeds
Soups: Cabbage, Asparagus & brown rice, Two pepper duet, Creamy fennel & orange, Tofu miso, Mangetout, mint & caviar, Seared salmon & wilted spinach, Fish with leek & spinach, Raw energy, Borscht, Fennel & tomato gazpacho, French onion, Minestrone, Ratatouille, Courgette & yellow pepper, Celeriac, leek & sage

Time to take stock

Home-made stocks make a lot of difference to any dish, particularly soups. The French call stock *fond de cuisine*, which, translated literally, means 'foundation of the kitchen'.

That said, you can buy a whole range of prepared bouillon cubes, packets of powdered stock and ready-made tubs of liquid stock. Always try to buy good-quality organic ones, so you can be sure that the ingredients are as nutritious as possible. The trouble with many ready-made stocks is their high salt content; take this into consideration and reduce the seasoning accordingly.

There is something immensely satisfying and therapeutic about making your own stock; you can add your own twists, it is more economical than buying stock and you can be sure of the origins and quality of your ingredients.

It just takes a little organization – if you go into the kitchen of any good restaurant, there are always a few stockpots on the go. Trimmings from vegetables, meat and fish go straight in and nothing is wasted. When faced with the sight of a chicken carcass about to be thrown away, I get palpitations and find myself standing at someone else's stove making stock, whether they want it or not. Whether making soups, or cooking a stir-fry, a drop or two of this essential ingredient makes all the difference.

It is much easier to make stock in bulk and freeze it, so always keep meat and fish trimmings in the freezer until you have enough to make a decent amount.

Individualize stocks by adding:
- Chillies for an extra kick
- Fennel seeds for aniseed overtones
- Ginger for bronchial clearing properties
- Dried mushrooms to intensify flavour
- Kaffir lime leaves to lend an Oriental citrus twist
- Soy sauce to darken and deepen the flavour
- Baked tomatoes and oregano for a Mediterranean feel
- Basil or tarragon for extra sweetness
- Star anise for liquorice overtones

Chicken stock

2–2½ kg (4–5 lb) chicken carcasses

2 onions, chopped

1 garlic bulb, chopped

3 large carrots, trimmed

3 leeks, chopped

5 celery sticks, chopped

1 lemon, halved

handful of flat leaf parsley

4 bay leaves

2 rosemary sprigs

1 teaspoon black peppercorns

6 litres (10 pints) water

If you are not a vegetarian, this stock is the most useful of all as it can intensify the flavour of most soups. For a satisfying light meal, boil a pan of chicken stock, add a few vegetables and a little chicken or fish, a splash of chilli oil and some extra lemon juice. This stock can be kept in the refrigerator for 2–3 days and can be frozen for 2–3 months.

1 Put all the ingredients into a large stockpot and bring slowly to the boil. Reduce the heat to a simmer and cook, covered, for 2 hours.
2 Remove the lid and simmer the stock for at least 1 more hour until it is a rich golden colour and the bones are clean, skimming as necessary.
3 Strain the stock, let it cool, then pour it into freezer containers if you are not using it immediately.

Makes 4 litres (7 pints)

Beef stock

Beef stock is a delicious broth that adds richness not only to meat-based soups but also to dishes such as borscht and even mushroom soup. Keep in the refrigerator for 2–3 days or freeze for 3–4 months.

1 Put the bones and meat into a large roasting tin, place in a preheated oven, 230°C (450°F), Gas Mark 8, and roast for 1 hour, turning regularly.
2 Add the carrots, onions, parsnips, celery, leek and garlic and roast for 20 minutes, making sure they don't burn.
3 Transfer the bones, meat and vegetables to a large stockpot and cover with most of the water. Deglaze the roasting tin over a medium heat with the remaining water then pour into the stockpot. Add the herbs and peppercorns and bring slowly to the boil, reduce the heat and simmer, covered, for 2 hours.
4 Remove the lid, then simmer the stock for another 3–4 hours. Skim off the fat when necessary.
5 Strain the stock, cool, then pour it into freezer containers.

5 kg (10 lb) beef bones and off-cuts

2 carrots, trimmed

4 onions, quartered

2 parsnips, trimmed

4 celery sticks, roughly chopped

1 leek, roughly chopped

1 garlic bulb, crushed

6 litres (10 pints) water

handful of parsley

2 bay leaves

2 teaspoons black peppercorns

Makes 4 litres (7 pints)

Fish stock

It is advisable not to use oily fish, such as herrings and mackerel, and imperative not to cook this stock for too long as it will become cloudy and the flavour will get very bitter. This stock can be kept in the refrigerator for 2–3 days or frozen for 2–3 months.

1 Remove the gills and eyes from any fish heads, if using, and wash all the bones thoroughly.
2 Heat the oil in a large heavy pan and sweat the vegetables and garlic, covered, for 5–6 minutes. Add the fish bones and trimmings and cook for a further 5 minutes.
3 Add the white wine, cold water and lemon juice and bring to the boil. Reduce the heat to a simmer, add the herbs and simmer gently for 20–30 minutes, skimming when necessary.
4 Strain the stock then let it cool. If you want to reduce the stock and intensify the flavour, simmer it gently until reduced by half, then allow to cool.

Makes 3 litres (5 pints)

2 kg (4 lb) fish trimmings

1 tablespoon olive oil

1 fennel bulb, roughly chopped

1 carrot, roughly chopped

3 celery sticks, roughly chopped

6 garlic cloves, roughly chopped

250 ml (8 fl oz) white wine

3 litres (5 pints) cold water

juice of 1 lemon

2 bay leaves

1 lemon thyme sprig

handful of parsley

Vegetable stock

This is a good all-purpose stock, which can be varied according to taste. You can make it spicier by adding ginger and chillies, while mushrooms and tomatoes will give it a more robust flavour. This stock can be kept in the refrigerator for up to 1 week or frozen for up to 3 months.

1 Heat the oil in a large stockpot and sweat all the vegetables and the garlic for 5–6 minutes.
2 Add the herbs, water, sea salt and peppercorns and bring to the boil, then lower the heat and simmer for 1½–2 hours, skimming occasionally.
3 Strain the stock through a sieve and let it cool.

Makes 3 litres (5 pints)

1 tablespoon olive oil

5 carrots, finely chopped

2 celery sticks with leaves, finely chopped

2 onions, finely chopped

2 leeks, finely sliced

1 fennel bulb, chopped

1 garlic bulb, unpeeled and roughly chopped

1 thyme sprig

1 rosemary sprig

1 bay leaf

handful of parsley

small bunch of basil

4 litres (7 pints) water

1 teaspoon sea salt

1 teaspoon black peppercorns

Clarifying stock

This technique is useful for adding extra flavour and lifting impurities from a stock. It is helpful when making consommés and clear broths.

3 egg whites, lightly beaten

3 crumbled egg shells

1 onion, very finely chopped

1 celery stick, very finely chopped

1 carrot, very finely chopped

handful of mixed herbs, finely chopped

Make sure the stock is at room temperature then pour it into a large pan. Mix all the ingredients in a bowl then whisk the mixture into the stock.

Bring the stock very slowly to a simmer, without stirring. As the sediments coagulate with the egg whites, a thick scum will rise to the surface of the liquid. Don't skim the stock – just push the scum aside so you can keep an eye on the liquid – it must not go above a simmer. Anything close to a boil will disturb the clarifying process. Simmer for about 10–15 minutes, then remove the pan from the heat and let it stand for 1 hour.

When you are ready to deal with the stock, dip a piece of muslin in hot water, wring it out and line a sieve. Push the scum aside and ladle the stock through the sieve.

Let the stock cool to room temperature, uncovered, then cover and refrigerate or freeze until required.

Clarifies 4 litres (7 pints) of stock

Freezing stock

To save space in your freezer, reduce ready-made stock to half the amount by boiling it vigorously, then freezing it in ice-cube trays and storing the ice cubes in plastic bags. To use, simply dissolve the stock in an equal amount of water, or add undiluted to soups and sauces for a more intense flavour.

souper boosters

Your immune system is your first line of defence against every toxin and germ the world throws at you. In order to function at optimum level the immune system needs proper nutrition to keep it strong and effective. If you have always got the sniffles or a cold, are prone to allergies, frequently feel stressed, use painkillers on a regular basis, suffer from headaches and sore throats, and drink alcohol more than three times a week – the chances are that your immune system is seriously overtaxed. The soups in this section are full of immune-boosting nutrients. You need to eat at least five portions of fruit and vegetables everyday to reinforce your defences. A bowl of one of these soups will provide at least one of those portions.

(Left: Gazpacho, see page 29 for recipe.)

Almond & broccoli soup

50 g (2 oz) ground almonds

625 g (1¼ lb) broccoli

900 ml (1½ pints) vegetable stock (see page 21)

300 ml (½ pint) soya milk

salt and pepper

This soup is full of vitamin C, which is essential when trying to build up the immune system after a long illness. The almonds and soya milk make this a good source of protein, while the calcium and zinc will help you to regain lost weight and strength. As a variation, this soup can be made with cauliflower and cashew nuts.

1 Spread the ground almonds on a baking sheet and toast in a preheated oven, 180°C (350°F), Gas Mark 4, for about 10 minutes until golden. Set aside one-quarter for the garnish.
2 Cut the broccoli into small florets and steam for 6–7 minutes over boiling water.
3 Place the remaining almonds, the broccoli, stock and soya milk in a food processor and blend until smooth. Season to taste then pour the purée into a pan and heat to a simmer.
4 Serve in warm bowls sprinkled with the reserved almonds.

Serves 4

200 kcals **13.5 g** protein **12.5 g** fat **8.3 g** carbs **218 mg** calcium **149 mg** vitamin C **1.74 mg** zinc

Fresh herb broth

The fresh green herbs added to this tasty broth at the last minute give it more than just a good flavour. They are packed with phytonutrients that will give your immune system a boost and, as they are alkaline, the soup will cleanse your blood and flush out your kidneys. You can vary the herbs to suit your taste – try thyme, basil, coriander, dill, wild rocket and oregano.

1 Set the herb leaves aside and put the stalks in a saucepan with the stock. Bring to a simmer and cook for 5 minutes then remove from the heat and leave to infuse for 15 minutes.
2 Melt the butter in a large saucepan and add the diced potato. Cover and cook over a gentle heat for 8 minutes, moistening the potato with a little stock if it begins to stick. Add the leek and cook for a few minutes more.
3 Bring the stock back to the boil then strain on to the vegetables. Cook over a medium heat until the vegetables are tender. Add a squeeze of lemon juice, if desired, and season to taste. Just before serving, stir in the chopped herbs.

Serves 4

161 kcals **13.5 g** carbs **11 g** fat **3 g** protein
58 mg calcium **52 mg** vitamin C

1 dessertspoon each of the following chopped herbs: flat leaf parsley, curly parsley, chervil, chives, tarragon and marjoram, stalks reserved

750 ml (1¼ pints) chicken or vegetable stock (see pages 19 and 21)

50 g (2 oz) butter

1 large potato, diced

1 large leek, finely sliced

squeeze of lemon juice (optional)

salt and pepper

Yellow tomato
gazpacho

1 kg (2 lb) ripe yellow tomatoes, skinned, deseeded and roughly chopped

½ cucumber, peeled, deseeded and roughly chopped

2 yellow peppers, cored, deseeded and roughly chopped

2 garlic cloves, crushed

1 small onion, roughly chopped

6 basil leaves, plus extra to garnish

2 tablespoons white wine vinegar

100 ml (3½ fl oz) olive oil

300 ml (½ pint) vegetable stock (see page 21)

1 tablespoon lemon juice

Tabasco sauce (optional)

salt and pepper

To garnish:

4 tablespoons Greek yogurt

4 tablespoons finely diced red pepper or red chillies

The vibrant colour of this delicious soup tells you that it is full of vitamin C, a natural antihistamine, making it a good anti-inflammatory choice for hayfever sufferers.

1 In a large bowl, mix together the tomatoes, cucumber, peppers, garlic, onion, basil, vinegar and olive oil and add a generous sprinkling of salt and pepper. Cover and leave in a cool place overnight to let the flavours mingle.

2 The next day, add the vegetable stock and lemon juice and blend the mixture in a food processor until smooth. Transfer to a bowl, cover and chill.

3 Season to taste and add a little Tabasco sauce if desired. Pour the soup into chilled bowls and garnish with a spoonful of Greek yogurt, a sprinkling of red pepper or chillies and a couple of basil leaves.

Serves 4

330 kcals 15 g carbs 27 g fat 5 g protein 64 mg calcium 134 mg vitamin C 4 mg vitamin E

Parsnip & pumpkin soup

1 tablespoon olive oil

15 g (½ oz) butter

1 onion, chopped

250 g (8 oz) carrots, chopped

250 g (8 oz) parsnips, chopped

250 g (8 oz) pumpkin, deseeded, skinned and chopped

900 ml (1½ pints) chicken or vegetable stock (see pages 19 and 21)

1–2 tablespoons lemon juice

salt and pepper

To garnish:

1 tablespoon olive oil

1 garlic clove, crushed

1 red chilli, deseeded and finely chopped

3 tablespoons chopped mixed parsley, mint and coriander

generous pinch of ground cumin

Foods with a naturally vibrant orange colour are full of alpha- and betacarotene. These powerful phytonutrients protect against many cancers and other degenerative diseases with their antioxidizing action. Both parsnips and pumpkin are also good for lowering blood pressure.

1 Heat the oil and butter in a large saucepan and fry the onion until soft. Add the carrots and parsnips and stir well. Cover the pan and cook over a gentle heat for 5 minutes. Add the pumpkin and cook, covered, for a further 5 minutes.

2 Pour in the stock and season with salt and pepper. Bring the stock to the boil, cover and simmer for 30 minutes, until all the vegetables are tender.

3 Leave to cool slightly, then blend in a food processor until smooth; if it is too thick, add a little extra water. Return the soup to the pan and reheat. Add lemon juice to taste.

4 Meanwhile, make the garnish. Heat the oil in a small pan, add the garlic, chilli, herbs and cumin and fry for 2 minutes.

5 To serve, pour the soup into warm bowls and spoon a little of the garnish on top.

Serves 4

140 kcals **14 g** carbs **8 g** fat **2.7 g** protein **50 mg** vitamin C **8 mg** betacarotene **96 mg** calcium

Gazpacho

1 kg (2 lb) ripe tomatoes, skinned, deseeded and roughly chopped

1 cucumber, peeled and roughly chopped

2 red peppers, cored, deseeded and roughly chopped

2 garlic cloves, crushed

175 g (6 oz) fresh white breadcrumbs

2 tablespoons white wine vinegar

2 tablespoons sun-dried tomato paste

6 tablespoons olive oil

salt and pepper

6–12 ice cubes, to serve

To garnish:

1 small avocado, peeled and cubed

½ cucumber, cut into 5 mm (¼ inch) cubes

2 hard-boiled eggs, roughly chopped

1 red onion, finely chopped

50 g (2 oz) pumpkin seeds

125 g (4 oz) cherry tomatoes, quartered

There are many versions of this refreshing, chilled, pungent soup from southern Spain (see page 22 for photograph), but the basic ingredients of raw tomatoes, peppers, cucumber and garlic provide an incredible burst of phytonutrients, vitamins and minerals that give a welcome boost to a flagging immune system. The raw garlic is a particularly powerful blood-thinner and is good for overall circulatory health. The tomatoes and tomato paste are rich in lycopene, which has been found to be an effective anticancer agent. Extra nutritional benefit is derived from the colourful raw garnish.

1 In a large bowl, mix together the tomatoes, cucumber, peppers, garlic, breadcrumbs, vinegar, tomato paste and olive oil. Season lightly with salt and pepper. Transfer to a food processor and blend until smooth. Cover and chill for several hours.
2 Mix together all the ingredients for the garnish. Serve the soup in bowls with 1 or 2 ice cubes and arrange the garnish in a separate bowl on the side.

Serves 6

437 kcals **35 g** carbs **28 g** fat **12 g** protein **96 mg** calcium **265 mg** phosphorus **70 mg** vitamin C

Creamy wild mushroom soup

This healthy version of creamy mushroom soup is ideal for people with high cholesterol as both mushrooms and garlic are well known as blood thinners. Shiitake mushrooms also have potent anticancer properties.

375 g (12 oz) mixed fresh wild mushrooms, such as morels, shiitake and oyster

1 tablespoon olive oil

1 onion, roughly chopped

1 potato, finely diced

1 litre (1¾ pints) chicken stock (see page 19)

2 garlic cloves, crushed

350 ml (12 fl oz) reduced-fat crème fraîche

salt and pepper

1 Chop the mushrooms very finely, reserving a few whole ones for the garnish.

2 Put half the oil into a heavy saucepan and cook the onion and potato gently for 10 minutes, or until the onion is translucent and the potato cooked through. Transfer the mixture to a food processor, cover with some of the stock and blend until smooth.

3 Put the chopped mushrooms and the whole mushrooms and garlic into the pan with the rest of the oil and sweat gently for about 5 minutes. Add the remaining stock and bring to the boil then reduce the heat to a simmer for a couple of minutes. Remove the whole mushrooms and reserve.

4 Gently combine the potato mixture with the crème fraîche in a large bowl. Remove the soup from the heat and add a ladleful of hot stock to the crème fraîche mixture, stirring briskly. Add another couple of ladlefuls, and stir carefully.

5 Return everything to the pan and mix thoroughly. Replace the pan on a very low heat and reheat gently. Season to taste and serve in warm bowls, garnished with the reserved mushrooms.

Serves 4

190 kcals **11 g** carbs **13 g** fat **9 g** protein **140 mg** calcium **200 mg** phosphorus

Mango, lime & ginger soup

2 large mangoes, peeled and diced

250 g (8 oz) Greek yogurt

1 tablespoon clear honey

juice of 1 lime

500 ml (17 fl oz) unsweetened white grape juice

½ teaspoon ground ginger

lime slices, pomegranate seeds or edible flowers, to garnish

This is a delicious soup bursting with betacarotene and vitamin C. Whenever you feel stressed and down, lighten your load with a bowlful of this fruity tonic that will cleanse your digestive system and kick-start your energy levels.

1 Put all the ingredients into a food processor and blend until smooth.
2 Transfer the purée to a bowl, cover and chill. Serve the soup in chilled bowls, and garnish with thin lime slices, pomegranate seeds or edible flowers.

Serves 4

180 kcals **30 g** carbs **6 g** fat **5 g** protein **1.4 mg** carotene
130 mg calcium **45 mg** vitamin C

Fresh tomato soup

1.5 kg (3 lb) ripe tomatoes

400 ml (14 fl oz) chicken or vegetable stock (see pages 19 and 21)

3 tablespoons sun-dried tomato paste

2–3 tablespoons balsamic vinegar

2–3 teaspoons raw brown sugar

small handful of basil leaves, plus extra to garnish

salt and pepper

crème fraîche, to garnish

This fresh-tasting soup is bursting with the phytonutrient lycopene, which is a powerful antioxidant, and protects against many types of cancer, particularly prostate. The advantage of lycopene is that it is not destroyed by the canning process and you can still find it in canned tomatoes and tomato products, so, if you haven't got fresh tomatoes, use an equal amount of canned.

1 Plunge the tomatoes into boiling water for 1 minute, then refresh in cold water. Peel away the skins and quarter the tomatoes then put them into a large saucepan and pour over the stock. Bring to the boil then reduce the heat and simmer gently for 10 minutes.
2 Stir in the tomato paste, vinegar, sugar and basil. Season with salt and pepper, then cook gently for 2 minutes.
3 Purée the soup in a food processor, then return it to the pan and reheat gently.
4 Serve the soup in warm bowls with a spoonful of crème fraîche and a few basil leaves.

Serves 6

60 kcals **2.4 g** protein **10.7 g** carbs **22.3 mg** calcium **1.3 g** fat **46 mg** vitamin C

Strawberry soup

875 g (1¾ lb) fresh organic strawberries

75 ml (3 fl oz) orange juice

75 ml (3 fl oz) white grape juice

75 g (3 oz) clear honey

2 tablespoons cornflour

50 ml (2 fl oz) cold water

1 teaspoon lemon juice

amaretti biscuits, broken, to decorate

Strawberries are antiviral, antibacterial and full of vitamin C, and they raise the levels of antioxidants in the body. This soup is a light, immune-boosting and decadent way to finish a meal.

1 Blend the strawberries in a food processor then pass the purée through a sieve to remove the seeds.
2 Combine the orange and grape juices, honey and sieved strawberries in a saucepan and heat gently until the honey has dissolved.
3 Mix the cornflour with the water and beat until no lumps remain. Pour into the hot soup, stirring continuously until the soup thickens. Add lemon juice to taste.
4 Pour the soup into small bowls and decorate with the chunks of amaretti biscuit.

Serves 4–6

100 kcals **24 g** carbs **1 g** protein **100 mg** vitamin C

Blueberry & oat soup

750 g (1½ lb) fresh
blueberries

600 ml (1 pint) water

150 g (5 oz) clear honey

3 tablespoons oatmeal

300 g (10 oz) Greek yogurt

pinch of salt

mint leaves, to garnish

Oats are renowned for lowering cholesterol while blueberries are full of polyphenols and flavonoids, which strengthen the blood vessels and reduce the risk of heart disease. This velvety soup makes an interesting starter or dessert.

1 Reserve a few blueberries for garnish. Put the rest into a saucepan with the water and honey and simmer for 10 minutes.
2 Blend the oatmeal in a food processor until it resembles fine flour. Whisk it into the yogurt with a pinch of salt.
3 Pour a little of the hot blueberry stock into the oatmeal mixture and whisk vigorously. Add this mixture to the remaining hot sweet stock and stir continuously for about 10 minutes whilst the soup slowly thickens.
4 Let the soup cool slightly then blend in a food processor until smooth. Transfer the soup to a bowl, cover the surface with plastic wrap and chill for about 1 hour. Serve in small bowls garnished with the mint leaves and reserved blueberries.

Serves 6

185 kcals **33 g** carbs **4.5 g** protein **4.5 g** fat **1.5 mg** iron **20 mg** vitamin C

Chamomile, cauliflower & lemon soup

Chamomile's subtlety and the sharpness of lemon juice do much to enhance the flavour of this soup. Cauliflower belongs to the cruciferous family which contains two prime disease-fighting ingredients. These are indole-3-carbinol (or I3C) and the phytonutrient sulforaphane, which gets rid of cancerous cells, preventing tumours before they begin. I3C works with the sulforaphane by acting as an antioestrogen. Cauliflower also contains vitamin C and folate, which helps the blood work more efficiently and is often recommended for preventing anaemia.

1 Put the stock and tea bags into a saucepan and boil for 5 minutes. Remove the tea bags, squeezing the excess liquid into the pan.
2 Add the cauliflower to the pan, cover and boil for 15 minutes, or until tender.
3 Melt the butter in a small frying pan and sauté the onion and celery until the onions are translucent. Transfer to a food processor or blender with the cauliflower and stock and blend until smooth. Pour the soup back into the pan, season and add lemon juice to taste.
4 Gently reheat and serve in warm bowls, garnished with chamomile flowers, chopped chives or lemon slices.

Serves 4

1.2 litres (2 pints) vegetable stock (see page 21)

6 chamomile tea bags

1 large cauliflower, trimmed and roughly chopped

25 g (1 oz) butter

1 onion, chopped

2 celery sticks, chopped

juice of 1 lemon

salt and pepper

chamomile flowers, chives or lemon slices, to garnish

122 kcals **7.8 g** carbs **7 g** fat **6 g** protein **95 mcg** folate **100 mcg** carotene **60 mg** vitamin C **600 mcg** vitamin E

Carrot & coriander soup

1 tablespoon olive oil

2 bay leaves

1 onion, roughly chopped

2 garlic cloves, chopped

625 g (1¼ lb) carrots, roughly chopped

small bunch of coriander, leaves separated from stems

1.2 litres (2 pints) vegetable stock (see page 21)

½ teaspoon garam masala

salt and pepper

4 tablespoons Greek yogurt or soya cream, to garnish

Carrots are a good source of betacarotene, calcium, phosphorus and magnesium and superb detoxifiers. They help to kill bacteria and viruses, so are an essential immune-boosting ingredient. There is a lot to be said for the old adage that carrots help your eyesight – they really do fight against macular degeneration.

1 Heat the oil in a saucepan, add the bay leaves, onion and garlic and fry for 2 minutes. Add the carrots, coriander stems and stock and bring to the boil. Simmer until the carrots are completely cooked.

2 Let the soup cool slightly, then remove the bay leaves and purée the soup in a food processor until smooth. If you like a very smooth soup, strain the soup back into the saucepan through a fine sieve; if not, just pour it all back into the pan and reheat gently. Season with salt, pepper and the garam masala. Finely chop half the coriander leaves and stir them into the soup.

3 Serve the soup in warm bowls and garnish with a tablespoon of Greek yogurt and the remaining coriander leaves.

Serves 4

131 kcals **14 g** carbs **7 g** fat **3.5 g** protein **118 mg** calcium **20 mg** carotene **32 mcg** folate **30 mg** magnesium **50 mg** phosphorus **16 mg** vitamin C

Spinach & watercress soup

1 tablespoon olive oil

1 onion, finely chopped

325 g (11 oz) potatoes, diced

600 ml (1 pint) chicken or vegetable stock (see pages 19 and 21)

250 g (8 oz) fresh or frozen spinach

75 g (3 oz) watercress

300 ml (½ pint) soya milk

salt

To garnish:

4 tablespoons natural yogurt

watercress sprigs

Spinach helps to clear wastes from the bowel and prevent constipation and diverticulitis. An excellent source of antioxidants, it has four times the betacarotene of broccoli. High in lutein, nutrients in spinach help lower blood cholesterol. It also contains vitamin A, vitamin C, calcium, iron and folic acid. Watercress belongs to the cruciferous vegetable family, known to be excellent sources of the cancer-fighting phytochemicals isothiocyanates.

1 Heat the oil in a large saucepan over a medium heat, add the onion and cook for 5–6 minutes until softened. Add the potatoes and stock and simmer for 15 minutes, until the potatoes are cooked.

2 Add the spinach, watercress and soya milk and simmer for 5 minutes. Remove the pan from the heat and let the soup cool slightly. Season with salt then purée in a food processor until smooth. Pour back into the pan and reheat gently.

3 Serve the soup in warm bowls, garnished with a tablespoon of yogurt and a watercress sprig.

Serves 4

166 kcals 24 g carbs 5 g fat 5 g protein
170 mg calcium 2.5 mg iron 120 mcg folate
40 mg vitamin C 510 mcg vitamin B6

Brussels sprout & chestnut soup

1 tablespoon olive oil

1 onion, finely chopped

1 celery stick, sliced

2 garlic cloves, chopped

500 g (1 lb) Brussels sprouts, trimmed and chopped

1.2 litres (2 pints) chicken stock (see page 19)

300 g (10 oz) canned chestnuts, drained and roughly chopped

1 teaspoon celery salt

nutmeg, to taste

salt and pepper

To garnish:

soured cream

chopped chives

Brussels sprouts contain many beneficial phytochemicals and are a good source of folate, vitamin C and iron. They also contain indoles which help protect against breast and colon cancer, and are antibacterial and antiviral. Chestnuts are rich in mineral salts and a good source of vitamins C, B1 and B2 and proteins and, like Brussels sprouts, they are full of fibre.

1 Heat the oil in a large saucepan and sauté the onion, celery and garlic over a medium heat for 5 minutes. Add the chopped Brussels sprouts and sauté for another 5 minutes.

2 Add the stock, bring to the boil and simmer, covered, for 10 minutes. Add the chestnuts and celery salt and cook for 5 minutes more.

3 Remove the pan from the heat and let it cool slightly. Blend the soup in a food processor until smooth. Pour the soup back into the pan, season with nutmeg, salt and pepper then reheat gently. Serve garnished with a drizzle of soured cream and a few chopped chives.

Serves 4

232 kcals 36 g carbs 7.5 g fat 6.7 g protein 178 mcg folate 150 mg vitamin C 820 mcg vitamin E

Seared salmon & wilted spinach soup

750 ml (1¼ pints) fish stock (see page 20)

1 teaspoon powdered saffron

1 teaspoon olive oil

2 spring onions, finely sliced

150 ml (5 fl oz) dry white wine

4 x 125 g (4 oz) salmon fillets with skin, cut lengthways into 2–3 strips

200 g (7 oz) baby spinach

2 limes, halved

salt and pepper

soy sauce, to serve

We should all be eating more fish, and this light yet nutrient-packed broth is a fantastic way to increase your levels of essential fatty acids. It is a delicate lunch dish that can be made more substantial with the addition of some rice or noodles, and it also has the immune-boosting properties of spinach and onions.

1 Bring the stock to the boil in a saucepan and add the saffron. Remove the pan from the heat and leave to infuse for 30 minutes.

2 Heat the oil in a saucepan over a medium heat, add the spring onions and sauté gently until soft. Add the white wine and boil until reduced by half. Pour in the stock and season with salt and pepper. Remove the pan from the heat until you are ready to serve.

3 Brush a griddle pan with a little oil and place over a medium heat for a couple of minutes. Cook the salmon strips skin-side down for about 1 minute, then turn and cook on the other side for 30–60 seconds. Set aside.

4 Gently reheat the stock. Put a couple of tablespoons into a pan with the spinach and cook over a high heat for about 1 minute, until the spinach has wilted.

5 Divide the spinach among 4 warm soup bowls. Place the salmon strips in the centre and pour over the hot stock. Serve with a lime half and offer soy sauce for drizzling.

Serves 4

324 kcals 2.5 g carbs 18 g fat 32 g protein 2.5 mg iron 90 mcg folate 12 mcg vitamin D
3 mg vitamin E 30 mg vitamin C

Souk soup

This chicken soup hails from the Islamic world. It is full of flavour and the apricots and oranges increase the betacarotene levels, giving a considerable boost to the immune system. Curcumin is a powerful compound in turmeric which has been the focus of recent research. It has been found to have antioxidant, anti-inflammatory and anticancer properties.

1 First make the spicy marinade. Put all the ingredients into a food processor and blend until the texture resembles a rough pesto sauce.
2 Put the chicken slices into a shallow dish and spread evenly with the marinade. Cover and chill overnight in the refrigerator.
3 Remove the chicken from the marinade and shake off any excess. Reserve the remaining marinade. Put the chicken into a large pan with half the oil and fry gently over a medium heat until evenly browned. Remove the chicken and set aside.
4 Add the remaining oil to the pan and fry the onion and fennel until softened. Add the remaining marinade, the tomatoes, apricots and chillies and cook for 2–3 minutes.
5 Add the stock to the pan. Return the chicken, stir, then simmer, covered, for 20 minutes. Add the orange segments and cook, uncovered, for 15 minutes.
6 Season to taste and serve in warm bowls garnished with mint leaves. Rice or couscous can be served on the side.

Serves 6

500 g (1 lb) chicken thighs, skinned, boned and sliced

2 tablespoons olive oil

200 g (7 oz) red onion, chopped

125 g (4 oz) fennel, finely sliced

6 tomatoes, skinned, deseeded and chopped

125 g (4 oz) dried apricots, finely sliced

2 small red chillies, deseeded and roughly chopped

1.5 litres (2½ pints) chicken stock (see page 19)

2 large oranges, segmented and roughly chopped

salt and pepper

mint leaves, to garnish

Spicy marinade:

25 g (1 oz) each mint, flat leaf parsley, coriander and basil, roughly chopped

1 teaspoon paprika

1 teaspoon ground turmeric

1 teaspoon ground cumin

½ teaspoon ground cinnamon

juice of 2 lemons

5 garlic cloves

2 tablespoons olive oil

380 kcals **20 g** carbs **14 g** fat **20 g** protein **120 mg** calcium **1.5 mg** iron **1.7 mg** carotene
55 mg vitamin C

Ratatouille soup

2 tablespoons olive oil

1 large onion, chopped

3 garlic cloves, chopped

1 small aubergine, chopped

1 courgette, chopped

1 yellow pepper, cored, deseeded and chopped

1 kg (2 lb) tomatoes, skinned, deseeded and chopped

2 tablespoons chopped basil

1 teaspoon chopped thyme or ¼ teaspoon dried thyme

500 ml (17 fl oz) vegetable or chicken stock (see pages 21 and 19)

pinch of cayenne pepper

salt and pepper

To garnish:

balsamic vinegar

shredded basil

This soup, which can be served hot or cold, is full of reinforcements for the immune system. Tomatoes contain a high level of antioxidants; they are also linked to a reduced risk of heart attacks and are a good source of vitamins C and E. Aubergines block the formation of free radicals, and onions and garlic are particularly effective against cold viruses.

1 Heat the oil in a large saucepan and sauté the onion and garlic for about 3 minutes over a medium heat, then add the aubergine, courgette and pepper and sauté, stirring from time to time, for another 5 minutes.

2 Stir in the tomatoes with their juice then stir in the herbs, stock and cayenne pepper. Season with salt and pepper and bring to the boil, then reduce the heat and simmer for 15–20 minutes.

3 To serve the soup hot and chunky, ladle it into bowls immediately. Spoon a little balsamic vinegar over each serving and sprinkle with basil.

4 To purée the soup, blend the solids in a food processor, then thin it with the broth, serve and garnish.

Serves 4

144 kcals 13 g carbs 8.5 g fat 4.5 g protein
75 mg vitamin C 2.5 mg vitamin E

high energy

Food provides the energy we need to carry out all our daily functions. Breathing, eating, walking, even thinking uses up precious fuel, and we often feel that we are lacking in energy even if we eat regularly. The answer lies in our choice of diet. If we are eating the wrong food, it could be robbing our bodies of that vital energy, particularly if it sends our blood sugar levels soaring up one moment and plummeting down the next. The key to blood sugar management is eating a good balance between carbohydrates, proteins and fats, with sufficient fibre to slow down digestion and keep glucose levels steady. This should come from slow-release carbohydrates such as whole grains, lean meat and fish, beans, pulses and healthy fats such as olive oil. It is essential to avoid processed and refined foods and a high intake of sugar, all of which will lead to a yo-yo energy cycle and increased fatigue.

(Right: Minestrone, see page 59 for recipe.)

Lentil & cumin soup

3 tablespoons vegetable oil

2 large onions, roughly chopped

4 garlic cloves, crushed

4 teaspoons cumin seeds

500 g (1 lb) dried green or brown lentils, rinsed

1 bay leaf

½ teaspoon dried oregano

3 litres (5 pints) chicken stock (see page 19)

150 ml (5 fl oz) soured cream, to garnish

Lentils provide an excellent source of minerals for nearly every organ in the body. They are especially effective when you are suffering from muscular fatigue as they neutralize the excess acids produced by weary muscles.

1 Heat 2 tablespoons of the oil in a saucepan and sauté the onion, garlic and 3 teaspoons of the cumin seeds for about 5 minutes, letting the onion brown and the cumin roast slightly.

2 Add the lentils, bay leaf, oregano and stock. Bring to the boil and simmer for about 35 minutes, or until the lentils are soft.

3 Remove the bay leaf, and purée the soup in a food processor. Blend all of the soup if you like a smooth texture, or if you prefer your soups a little chunkier, only blend half then stir it back into the unblended part.

4 Heat the remaining oil in a small pan and sauté the remaining cumin seeds over a medium heat for about 1 minute, or until they are slightly crisp. Drain on kitchen paper.

5 Serve the soup in warm bowls garnished with a tablespoon of soured cream and a sprinkling of the roast cumin seeds.

Serves 10

254 kcals **28 g** carbs **10.5 g** fat **14 g** protein **90 mg** calcium **70 mg** magnesium **2.25 mg** zinc

49

Black bean soup

This robust soup is packed with fibre and is very good for cleansing the digestive tract. Beans are excellent for sustained energy and have a cholesterol-lowering effect on the bloodstream.

1 Drain and rinse the beans three times and allow to dry.
2 Put the olive oil, onion and garlic in a large saucepan and sweat gently, covered, for about 5 minutes.
3 Add the beans and stock and bring to the boil then reduce the heat to a simmer. Add the celery, carrot, thyme, bay leaves, cloves and mace and cook for 1½ hours, or until the beans are soft.
4 Let the mixture cool slightly, then purée in a food processor or blender until smooth, discarding the herbs.
5 Return the soup to the pan and reheat it, then season with salt and pepper. Serve in warm bowls with a spoonful of soured cream, and a sprinkling of chillies and coriander.

Serves 6

200 g (7 oz) dried black-eyed beans, soaked in water overnight

3 tablespoons olive oil

1 onion, finely chopped

1 garlic clove, crushed

2 litres (3½ pints) vegetable stock (see page 21)

1 celery stick, sliced

1 large carrot, sliced

2 thyme sprigs

2 bay leaves

a pinch each of ground cloves and mace

salt and pepper

To garnish:

4 tablespoons soured cream

2 chilli peppers, deseeded and finely diced

1 tablespoon chopped coriander leaves

236 kcals **23 g** carbs **11 g** fat **11 g** protein **74 mg** calcium **12 mg** vitamin C

Curried parsnip & apple soup

1 teaspoon coriander seeds

1 teaspoon cumin seeds

seeds from 6 cardamom pods

40 g (1½ oz) butter

1 tablespoon groundnut oil

2 onions, chopped

2 garlic cloves, chopped

1 teaspoon ground ginger

1 teaspoon turmeric

750 g (1½ lb) young parsnips, diced

1.2 litres (2 pints) chicken or vegetable stock (see pages 19 and 21)

1 Bramley apple

salt and pepper

To garnish:

chopped coriander leaves

dry-roasted cumin seeds

This sweet rich soup is based on the potent partnership of parsnips and apples. They are both excellent for detoxifying the digestive system and stimulating regular bowel movement.

1 Dry-roast the coriander, cumin and cardamom seeds in a small frying pan for 2–3 minutes, or until they are browned and jumping in the pan. Crush using a pestle and mortar.
2 Heat the butter and oil in a saucepan until the butter froths, then add the onions and soften for 5 minutes over a gentle heat.
3 Add the garlic and cook for 2 minutes. Add the crushed spices, ginger and turmeric. Add the parsnips and stock and simmer for 1 hour, uncovered.
4 Remove the soup from the heat and blend in a food processor. Return to the pan, check the seasoning and simmer until heated through.
5 Peel the apple and grate it into the soup, cook for 2 minutes then pour the soup into warm bowls. Garnish with a little chopped coriander and cumin seeds and serve.

Serves 6

204 kcals 24 g carbs 10 g fat 4.3 g protein 91 mg calcium
46 mg magnesium 120 mg phosphorus 28 mg vitamin C 1.7 mg vitamin E

Chickpea & parsley soup

Chickpeas provide complex carbohydrates which release energy slowly into the bloodstream, keeping energy levels consistent. They are rich in magnesium and potassium, while parsley is a very good source of vitamin C. These nutrients are extremely useful for people suffering from any form of kidney disease, as conventional treatments can often deplete the body of essential vitamins and minerals.

1 Drain the chickpeas and rinse under running cold water. Cook in boiling water for 10 minutes, then simmer for 45–60 minutes until just tender.

2 Place the onion, garlic and parsley in a food processor and blend until finely chopped.

3 Heat the oil in a large saucepan and cook the onion mixture over a low heat until slightly softened. Add the chickpeas and cook gently for 1–2 minutes, then pour in the stock, season well with salt and pepper and bring to the boil. Cover the pan and cook for 20 minutes, or until the chickpeas are really tender.

4 Let the soup cool for a while, then part-purée in a blender, or mash with a fork, so that it still has plenty of texture.

5 Return the soup to a clean pan, add the lemon juice and taste for seasoning. Serve in warm bowls topped with grated lemon rind and cracked black pepper.

Serves 4

250 g (8 oz) dried chickpeas, soaked overnight in water

1 small onion

3 garlic cloves

40 g (1½ oz) parsley

2 tablespoons olive oil

1.2 litres (2 pints) vegetable stock (see page 21)

juice of ½ lemon

salt and pepper

To garnish:

grated lemon rind

cracked black pepper

286 kcals **32 g** carbs **13.5 g** protein **12 g** fat **110 mg** calcium **98 mg** magnesium **24 mg** vitamin C

Chunky barley, bean & peanut butter soup

125 g (4 oz) pearl barley

1 litre (1¾ pints) vegetable stock (see page 21)

1 tablespoon olive oil

2 garlic cloves, chopped

1 small green chilli, deseeded and finely chopped

1 green pepper, cored, deseeded and finely chopped

½ teaspoon ground cumin

½ teaspoon paprika

175 g (6 oz) canned chopped tomatoes

125 g (4 oz) spinach, sliced

250 g (8 oz) canned refried beans

½ teaspoon dried oregano

50 g (2 oz) frozen sweetcorn kernels

50 g (2 oz) green beans, finely sliced

50 g (2 oz) carrots, diced

50 g (2 oz) fennel, finely chopped

50 g (2 oz) red pepper, cored, deseeded and finely chopped

2 tablespoons chunky peanut butter

salt and pepper

3 tablespoons chopped coriander leaves, to garnish

Don't be put off by the long list of ingredients – this soup is very simple to make. The nutritional value of the vegetables remains high as they are added to the soup just 5 minutes before serving. Barley, beans and peanuts ensure the soup is full of B vitamins and provide many essential amino acids, while the tomatoes and spinach provide an extra punch of vitamin C. This is a great soup if you suffer from high cholesterol as it contains many of the ingredients that are associated with keeping LDL (bad cholesterol) levels low.

1 Put the barley in a large saucepan with half of the vegetable stock. Bring to the boil and simmer for about 30 minutes until the barley is tender. Drain the barley and pour back the excess cooking liquid into the remaining stock.

2 Heat the oil and lightly sauté the garlic until it has softened, then add the chilli, green pepper, cumin and paprika. Cook for a few minutes, then add the tomatoes, stock and spinach and simmer for 10 minutes.

3 Add the refried beans, stir thoroughly and add the oregano, sweetcorn kernels, green beans, carrots, fennel, red pepper and peanut butter. Cook for another 5–6 minutes, or until the vegetables are just cooked through.

4 Season with salt and pepper then transfer to warm bowls and garnish with the chopped coriander.

Serves 4

325 kcals **39 g** carbs **12 g** fat **13 g** protein **120 mg** magnesium
6 mg iron **120 mg** calcium **90 mg** vitamin C **300 mcg** vitamin B6

Moroccan harira

Traditionally this hearty meat and vegetable soup is eaten during the month of Ramadan, when Muslims fast between sunrise and sunset. It is full of goodness and is hugely nourishing. It has a good balance between protein, carbohydrate and fats, which is great for slow energy release. Canned chickpeas can be used instead of dried ones. Add 175 g (6 oz) canned chickpeas with the baby onions and reduce the water to 450 ml (¾ pint).

1 Put the lamb, turmeric, cinnamon, butter, coriander, parsley and onion into a large saucepan and cook over a medium heat for 5 minutes, stirring continuously. Add the chopped tomatoes and continue cooking for 10 minutes.

2 Rinse the lentils under running cold water and add to the pan with the drained chickpeas and the water. Season with salt and pepper. Bring to the boil, cover and simmer gently for 1½ hours. If using canned chickpeas, reduce the time to 1 hour.

3 Add the baby onions and cook for 30 minutes. Serve garnished with coriander, lemon slices and cinnamon.

Serves 4

300 kcals **23 g** carbs **14 g** fat **20 g** protein **100 mg** calcium **4.5 mg** iron **4 mg** zinc

250 g (8 oz) lean lamb, cut into 1 cm (½ inch) cubes

½ teaspoon ground turmeric

½ teaspoon ground cinnamon

25 g (1 oz) butter

4 tablespoons chopped coriander leaves

2 tablespoons chopped parsley

1 onion, chopped

500 g (1 lb) tomatoes, skinned and roughly chopped

50 g (2 oz) split red lentils

75 g (3 oz) dried chickpeas, soaked overnight

600 ml (1 pint) water

4 baby onions or shallots

salt and pepper

To garnish:

chopped coriander leaves

lemon slices

ground cinnamon

Prawn & scallop laksa

500 g (1 lb) raw shell-on tiger prawns

1.5 litres (2½ pints) water

1 tablespoon vegetable oil

200 g (7 oz) thin rice noodles

500 ml (17 fl oz) coconut milk

8 large scallops, without roes, sliced into 3 discs

Spice paste:

4–5 large dried chillies

1 red onion, roughly chopped

5 cm (2 inch) piece of fresh galangal or root ginger, peeled and roughly chopped

4 lemon grass stalks, white part only, sliced

3 fresh red chillies, deseeded and roughly chopped

10 macadamia nuts or cashews

2 teaspoons shrimp paste

2 teaspoons grated fresh turmeric or ½ teaspoon ground turmeric

2 tablespoons vegetable oil

To garnish:

mint leaves

lemon or lime wedges

This healthy soup is so delicious that it is worth the effort of making from scratch rather than buying a ready-made version. The flavour is wonderful, and contains many nutritious ingredients that will act as a brain booster. The coconut will help counter any thyroid imbalance and normalize metabolism.

1 First make the spice paste. Soak the dried chillies in hot water for 20 minutes, drain and put into a food processor with the remaining spice paste ingredients. Process in short bursts, regularly scraping the sides of the bowl with a spatula to ensure all the ingredients are very finely chopped.

2 Peel and devein the prawns, reserving the heads and shells. Put the heads and shells into a heavy pan and cook over a medium heat for 10 minutes until they have turned dark orange. Stir in 250 ml (8 fl oz) of the water and, when it has almost evaporated, add another 250 ml (8 fl oz) and bring to the boil. Then add the remaining water, bring to the boil and simmer for 30 minutes – this slow process ensures the stock will be dark and full of flavour. Strain the stock and discard the heads and shells.

3 Heat the oil in a wok and cook the spice paste over a low heat for about 7 minutes, stirring regularly, until the mixture is very aromatic.

4 Put the rice noodles to soak in a large bowl of boiling water.

5 Add the prawn stock and coconut milk to the spice paste. Bring to the boil and simmer for 8 minutes. Add the peeled prawns, cook for 2 minutes, then add the sliced scallops and cook for a further 2 minutes.

6 Drain the noodles and divide among 4 deep warm soup bowls. Place a selection of prawns and scallop slices on top of the noodles, pour over some of the hot stock, then garnish with the mint and lemon or lime wedges.

Serves 4

630 kcals 58 g carbs 25 g fat 38 g protein 6 mg iron 4 mg zinc

Algerian wheat soup

2 tablespoons olive oil, plus extra to garnish

1 onion, chopped

4 garlic cloves, chopped

1 teaspoon paprika

pinch of cayenne pepper

125 ml (4 fl oz) tomato purée

1 litre (1¾ pints) vegetable stock (see page 21)

50 g (2 oz) bulgur wheat

1 tablespoon chopped parsley

1 tablespoon chopped coriander leaves

1 tablespoon chopped mint

50 g (2 oz) canned chickpeas

1–2 tablespoons lemon juice

salt and pepper

This simple soup is the vegetarian equivalent of the Moroccan Harira, and is also eaten during the month of Ramadan. Its combination of wheat and chickpeas provides the optimum vegetarian supply of protein gained from eating grains and pulses together. It is rich in B vitamins and is a perfect energy-boosting soup.

1 Heat the oil in a large saucepan and sauté the onion until softened, then stir in the garlic, paprika and cayenne. Cook for 2 minutes, stirring continuously.

2 Add the tomato purée and stock, bring to a simmer and add the bulgur. Cover, and simmer for 30 minutes, stirring occasionally, until the bulgur is tender.

3 Let the soup cool slightly then add the parsley, coriander and mint, reserving ½ tablespoon for the garnish, and blend in a food processor until you have a rough texture.

4 Return the soup to the pan. Stir in the chickpeas and heat through. Ladle into warm bowls and add the lemon juice and season with salt and pepper. Sprinkle with the reserved herbs and drizzle with extra olive oil.

Serves 4

200 kcals 23 g carbs 9 g fat 6 g protein
175 mcg vitamin B1 35 mg vitamin C 2.5 mg iron

Minestrone

3 tablespoons olive oil

125 g (4 oz) rindless pancetta, roughly chopped

3 celery sticks, finely chopped

3 carrots, finely chopped

1 onion, finely chopped

3 garlic cloves, finely chopped

400 g (13 oz) can chopped tomatoes

1 litre (1¾ pints) chicken stock (see page 19)

50 g (2 oz) brown rice

425 g (14 oz) can cannellini beans, drained and rinsed

4 tablespoons flat leaf parsley, chopped

salt and pepper

Parmesan shavings, to serve

There are a million ways to make minestrone, but whatever version you prefer, the ingredients always include tomatoes, onions, garlic, olive oil, beans, some form of grain such as pasta or rice, and a delicious sprinkling of Parmesan cheese. I always make mine with pancetta or unsmoked bacon, and chicken stock, as I love the robust flavour, but if you prefer a vegetarian version, simply omit the pancetta, and use vegetable stock. Whatever your method, this soup is full of nutrients and is a meal in itself. (See page 46 for photograph.)

1 Gently heat the oil in a large saucepan, add the pancetta and cook for 1 minute then add the celery, carrots and onion and fry for a few minutes to soften.
2 Add the garlic and tomatoes and stir, then add the stock. Season with salt and pepper to taste. Bring to the boil then reduce the heat and simmer for 10 minutes.
3 Add the rice and simmer for a further 10 minutes then add the beans and bring back to the boil. Cover the pan, lower the heat and cook for 20 minutes more. If the soup looks too dry, add more stock.
4 Stir in half the parsley and serve hot, sprinkled with the remaining parsley and some Parmesan cheese.

Serves 6

207 kcal 25 g carbo 17 g fat 10.5 g protein 140 mcg calcium 3.2 mcg iron 40 mg vitamin C

Sweet potato soup
with coconut & lime cream

Sweet potato is the richest low-fat source of vitamin E, which is vital for energy production and cellular respiration. It contributes to heart health and is a good source of dietary antioxidants, particularly betacarotene. It can help to regulate high blood pressure and also helps anaemia. It may also protect against inflammatory conditions and is attributed with anti-ageing properties.

1 Heat the oil in a large saucepan over a medium heat and sauté the onion, garlic, ginger and curry powder until the onion is translucent.
2 Add the chopped sweet potato and cook for 1–2 minutes without browning it. Add the stock, cover and cook for 10 minutes, or until the sweet potato is tender.
3 Purée the soup in a food processor then return it to the pan and gently reheat. Season to taste.
4 To make the coconut and lime cream, mix together the coconut cream, lime juice and lime rind. Ladle the soup into bowls and garnish with a generous drizzle of the cream.

Serves 4

1 tablespoon olive oil

1 onion

2 garlic cloves

1 teaspoon finely grated fresh root ginger

1 teaspoon medium curry powder

500 g (1 lb) sweet potato, peeled and diced

1 litre (1¾ pints) vegetable or chicken stock (see pages 21 and 19)

salt and pepper

Coconut and lime cream:

150 ml (¼ pint) coconut cream

juice of ½ lime

1 teaspoon grated lime rind

294 kcals 32 g carbs 17.5 g fat 4 g protein 6 mg vitamin E 36 mg vitamin C 5 mg carotene 28 mcg folate

stress busting and brain boosters

Stress comes in many forms, physical and mental; in fact, it includes anything that disturbs the body's delicate natural balance. Pollution, smoking, excessive alcohol, a heavy workload, emotional problems, food intolerances, blood sugar imbalances, hormonal disturbance and nutritional deficiencies all put our bodies under immense pressure and can lead to physical and mental breakdown, predisposing us to degenerative diseases and making us susceptible to infection. These soups will maintain the delicate balance of the hormones cortisol and DHEA (dehydroepiandosterone) by providing essential nutrients for the effective functioning of the adrenal glands, boosting the immune system, soothing the digestive tract and having a calming effect on the body.

(Right: Mushy pea & ham soup, see page 76 for recipe.)

Fish soup
with leek & spinach

300 g (10 oz) fish fillets, such as salmon, mackerel or tuna

1 tablespoon olive oil

1.5 cm (¾ inch) piece of fresh root ginger, peeled and cut into fine strips

1 leek, finely sliced

125 g (4 oz) baby spinach leaves, washed

3 tablespoons finely chopped spring onion

2 tablespoons chopped chervil

900 ml (1½ pints) fish or vegetable stock (see pages 20 and 21)

salt and pepper

This light and delicate combination of oily fish and spinach is excellent brain food. The fish is packed with omega-3 fatty acids which are essential for peak performance as the brain is predominantly made of fat, and almost all of its structures and functions are dependant on essential fatty acids, which we get directly from our foods.

1 Cut the fish into very fine slices.
2 Heat the oil in a small frying pan and stir-fry the ginger and leek for 3 minutes.
3 Place the spinach in the bottom of a soup tureen or individual serving bowls. Add the leek and ginger and arrange the fish slices on top. Season with a little salt and pepper and sprinkle with the spring onion and chervil.
4 Bring the stock to the boil and pour over the fish and other ingredients. This will cook the fish immediately, so serve it straight away.

Serves 4

74 kcals **3.3 g** carbs **5.6 g** fat **3 g** protein **72 mg** calcium **22 mg** magnesium
30 mg vitamin C

Chilled avocado & palm heart soup

3 large avocados, peeled, stoned and cut into chunks

juice of 1 lemon

500 g (1 lb) natural yogurt

250 g (8 oz) canned palm hearts

a few drops of Tabasco sauce

500 ml (17 fl oz) vegetable stock (see page 21)

2 teaspoons chopped coriander leaves

salt and pepper

To garnish:

coriander leaves

finely chopped tomatoes

spring onions

Many nutritionists describe avocados as the perfect food because their acid-alkaline content is balanced, making them easily digested. They are high in many essential minerals and vitamins, especially vitamin E which is a powerful antioxidant and vital for healthy blood flow. This light, yet satisfying soup is a perfect summer lunch dish that will cool and soothe the digestive tract.

1 Place the avocado chunks in a food processor and sprinkle with the lemon juice.
2 Add all the remaining ingredients and process until smooth. Cover and chill for at least 1 hour before serving.
3 Serve in chilled bowls and garnish with coriander leaves, finely chopped tomatoes and spring onions.

Serves 4

381 kcals 11.5 g carbs 34 g fat 10 g protein 5 mg vitamin E 14.5 mg vitamin C 200 mg calcium 1.5 mg zinc

Mussel & coconut soup

Seafood is universally hailed as brain food and, as it is high in zinc, it is a beneficial addition to the diet when stress levels are high and you have been burning the candle at both ends. Zinc helps to break down alcohol and is a vital component of insulin, which controls blood sugar levels.

1 Wash the mussels in running cold water. Pull off their hairy beards and discard any mussels that are open and do not close when tapped.

2 Put the wine and shallots into a large saucepan and boil for about 2–3 minutes. Add the mussels and boil for 2 minutes, or until all the mussels have opened. Immediately tip the mussels into a colander with a bowl underneath to catch juices.

3 As soon as the mussels are cool enough to handle, carefully pull them from their shells, discarding any that have not opened. Reserve the broth and the mussels.

4 Strain the mussel broth into a large pan, discarding any grit or dirt that may have sunk to the bottom. Add the coconut milk, ginger, tomatoes, chillies and sweetcorn. Heat and simmer for 2 minutes, then add the mussels.

5 Serve the soup in warm bowls sprinkled with spring onion and basil leaves.

Serves 6

1½ kg (3 lb) mussels

150 ml (¼ pint) dry white wine

4 shallots, finely chopped

1 litre (1¾ pints) canned coconut milk

½ tablespoon finely chopped fresh root ginger

3 plum tomatoes, skinned, deseeded and roughly chopped

2 large chillies, deseeded and chopped

4 tablespoons cooked sweetcorn kernels

To garnish:

1 spring onion, finely sliced

2 tablespoons basil leaves

154 kcals **16 g** carbs **3 g** fat **13 g** protein **23 mg** vitamin C **85 mg** magnesium **92 mg** calcium **2 mg** zinc

Armenian soup

This lentil-based soup provides a good source of vitamins B5 and B6, which are vital for healthy adrenal function and energy production. It is also very high in calcium, which is a natural tranquillizer so, if you are overworked and stressed out, this soup would be a healthy choice to help keep your body going.

1 Put all the ingredients into a large saucepan and bring to the boil. Cover the pan and simmer for 30 minutes.
2 Let the soup cool, then blend in a food processor until smooth.
3 Reheat the soup and serve in warm bowls with a sprinkling of roasted cumin seeds and a few slivers of orange rind.

Serves 4

50 g (2 oz) red lentils

50 g (2 oz) dried apricots

1 large potato, roughly chopped

1.2 litres (2 pints) vegetable or chicken stock (see pages 21 and 19)

juice of 1 lemon

1 teaspoon ground cumin

3 tablespoons chopped parsley

salt and pepper

To garnish:

roasted cumin seeds

slivers of orange rind

420 kcals **85 g** carbs **4.7 g** fat **22 g** protein **318 mg** calcium **20 mg** iron **1.5 mg** vitamin B6 **2 mg** vitamin B5 **120 mg** vitamin C **400 mg** phosphorus **175 mg** magnesium

Earth apple soup

I have called this soup after the French word for potato, *pomme de terre*, which means apple of the earth. Potatoes are particularly good for anyone suffering from high blood pressure as they are high in potassium, which balances sodium levels in the body. It is also a good dish for anyone who has been relying on stimulants such as alcohol and coffee – both these will deplete the body of potassium, a deficiency which can lead to all manner of ailments.

1 Put the potatoes and stock into a large saucepan, bring to the boil and simmer, covered, for 15 minutes, or until the potatoes are cooked.
2 Meanwhile, heat the oil in a saucepan and sauté the leeks for 10 minutes, then add the orange rind, turmeric, fennel seeds and bacon and cook for 5–6 minutes.
3 When the potatoes are cooked, drain them through a sieve over a bowl and pour the stock into the leek mixture. Season with salt and pepper.
4 Mash the potatoes, add half to the stock mixture and stir well. Add the egg yolk, nutmeg and parsley to the rest of the potato and mix thoroughly. Put the mash into a piping bag and pipe a mound of mashed potato into each warm serving bowl.
5 Pour the soup around the potato mounds and sprinkle with chopped chives and a grinding of black pepper.

Serves 8

1 kg (2 lb) potatoes, peeled and cut into 2.5 cm (1 inch) cubes

1.5 litres (2½ pints) chicken or vegetable stock (see pages 19 and 21)

2 tablespoons olive oil

4 leeks, finely sliced

pared rind of 1 orange, in 1 piece

1 teaspoon ground turmeric

1 teaspoon fennel seeds

4 rindless bacon rashers, cut into fine strips

1 egg yolk

½ teaspoon ground nutmeg

2 tablespoons finely chopped parsley

salt and pepper

2 tablespoons chopped chives, to garnish

255 kcals **34 g** carbs **9.5 g** fat **11 g** protein **800 mg** potassium **50 mg** magnesium **92 mg** calcium **40 mg** vitamin C

Hot & sour
prawn soup

A bowlful of this fiery soup will help fend off a chesty cough, as chillies pack a powerful bronchial-clearing punch. It is excellent for clearing mucus, which can build up when the body has been taking in too many toxins. So, if you are feeling run down, stop any imminent infection in its tracks.

1 Peel and devein the prawns, leaving the tails intact.
2 Heat the oil in a saucepan and cook the prawn shells for 8–10 minutes, until the shells are deep orange. Add 250 ml (8 fl oz) of the water and the curry paste to the pan. Boil for 5 minutes until reduced slightly. Add the remaining water and simmer for 20 minutes. Drain the stock, discarding the heads and shells.
3 Return the drained stock to the pan. Add the tamarind, turmeric, chilli and lime leaves, bring to the boil and cook for 2 minutes. Add the prawns to the pan and cook for 5 minutes or until they turn pink. Add the fish sauce, lime juice and sugar and stir well.
4 Serve the soup immediately, sprinkled with coriander leaves.

Serves 6

500 g (1 lb) raw shell-on tiger prawns

1 tablespoon vegetable oil

2 litres (3½ pints) water

2 tablespoons Thai red curry paste

2 tablespoons tamarind concentrate

2 tablespoons ground turmeric

1 teaspoon chopped red chilli

4–8 kaffir lime leaves

2 tablespoons Thai fish sauce

2 tablespoons lime juice

2 teaspoons soft brown sugar

handful of coriander leaves, to garnish

142 kcals 8 g carbs 5.5 g fat 15.5 g protein 88 mg calcium 3.5 mg iron 1.45 mg zinc

Silken tofu & lettuce soup

Lettuce aids digestion and promotes liver health. It can also reduce the risk of heart disease, strokes and cataracts and helps to counteract the risk of cancer. It is also said to prevent spina bifida and anaemia and, because it contains the natural sedative lactucarium, it encourages restful sleep.

1 Heat the oil in a saucepan and sauté the onion and garlic for 5 minutes.
2 Add the stock, bring to the boil and simmer for 2 minutes. Add the lettuce, rocket, parsley and tarragon and simmer for 15 minutes.
3 Put the silken tofu into a food processor or blender and add 2 ladlefuls of the hot stock. Blend until smooth.
4 Pour the blended tofu back into the soup and season with salt and pepper. Reheat the soup and serve with a drizzle of sour cream, if liked.

Serves 4

1 tablespoon olive oil

1 onion, finely chopped

2 garlic cloves, crushed

1.2 litres (2 pints) vegetable stock (see page 21)

200 g (7 oz) Cos lettuce, finely shredded

100 g (3½ oz) rocket, finely chopped

2 tablespoons finely chopped parsley

1 tablespoon finely chopped tarragon

250 g (8 oz) silken tofu

salt and pepper

soured cream, to garnish (optional)

130 kcals **6.7 g** carbs **8 g** fat **7.7 g** protein **400 mg** calcium **30 mg** vitamin C

Indonesian chicken & peanut soup

1 litre (1¾ pints) chicken stock (see page 19)

2 tablespoons soy sauce

1½ tablespoons molasses

2 tablespoons lemon juice

2 garlic cloves

40 g (1½ oz) smooth peanut butter

50 g (2 oz) unsalted peanuts, chopped

125 g (4 oz) cooked chicken, shredded

75 g (3 oz) spring onions, finely sliced

Molasses is made from sugar cane. The roots of the sugar cane grow as deep as 4.5 metres (15 feet) and receive a broad spectrum of minerals and trace elements normally lacking in the top soils. During the refining process – when the white sugar is taken away – it leaves a molasses, an exceptionally rich mineral/trace element cocktail, that is particularly high in magnesium which supports the adrenals. Peanuts contain the phytochemical resveratrol, which has been linked to a significant decrease in heart disease. Peanuts have anticancer effects and can also lower cholesterol levels if they are eaten in place of other high-fat foods.

1 Combine the stock, soy sauce, molasses, lemon juice and garlic in a large saucepan. Bring to the boil then reduce the heat and simmer, uncovered, for about 15 minutes.
2 Whisk in the peanut butter and simmer for 5 minutes.
3 When you are ready to serve, stir in the peanuts, chicken and spring onions. Heat through, then ladle into warm soup bowls. Serve immediately.

Serves 4

208 kcals 9.5 g carbs 11.5 g fat 16.5 g protein 2 mg vitamin E 1.5 mg iron 23 mcg folate

73

Sicilian tuna soup

50 g (2 oz) can anchovies

1 tablespoon olive oil, plus extra to drizzle

1 onion, finely chopped

2 garlic cloves, finely chopped

1 courgette, diced

400 g (13 oz) can chopped tomatoes

1 litre (1¾ pints) chicken stock (see page 19)

2 tablespoons dry sherry

75 g (3 oz) each black and green pitted olives, finely sliced

425 g (14 oz) canned cannellini beans, drained

400 g (13 oz) fresh tuna, cut into 2.5 cm (1 inch) cubes

juice of 1 lemon

25 g (1 oz) oregano leaves

25 g (1 oz) basil, roughly torn

salt and pepper

crusty bread, to serve

This meal in a bowl contains all the best and most healthy ingredients that form the basis of the Mediterranean diet – olives, tomatoes, garlic, onions, oily fish and fresh herbs. It is a celebration of healthy fats – and includes plenty of omega-3 fatty acids. You can taste the sunshine, and your brain, heart, circulation and immune system will love it.

1 Drain the oil from the anchovies into a large saucepan, add the olive oil and warm over a medium heat. Add the onion, garlic and courgette and sauté until the onion is transparent.

2 Finely chop the anchovies and add to the pan with the chopped tomatoes, stock, sherry and olives. Season with pepper and a little salt if necessary and simmer over a low heat for 15 minutes.

3 Add the beans and tuna and simmer for a further 15 minutes.

4 Just before serving, add lemon juice to taste and transfer the soup to a large serving bowl. Sprinkle with the oregano and basil and serve with crusty bread and extra olive oil to drizzle.

Serves 4

412 kcals 26 g carbs 17 g fat 38 g protein 7 mg iron 40 mcg folate 30 mg vitamin C 235 mg calcium

Mushy pea & ham soup

1 meaty ham bone, with about 500 g (1 lb) ham

1.5 litres (2½ pints) chicken stock (see page 19)

625 g (1¼ lb) green split peas, soaked overnight in water and drained

1 litre (1¾ pints) water

2 onions, finely chopped

2 leeks, finely sliced

2 celery sticks, finely sliced

2 potatoes, diced

1 teaspoon chopped thyme

½ teaspoon caraway seeds

½ teaspoon ground nutmeg

1 tablespoon lemon juice

salt and pepper

thyme sprigs, to garnish

This soup is a powerhouse of restorative nutrients and will help you to recover. It is full of both protein and carbohydrates so will ensure slow-release sustainable energy. Peas are a very good source of vitamin B1, the morale vitamin. B1 is essential for a healthy nervous system and is linked to improving learning capacity. It is also essential for the conversion of glucose to energy. (See page 62 for photograph.)

1 Put the ham bone, water and stock into a large saucepan. Bring to the boil then reduce the heat and simmer, covered, for 1 hour.

2 Add the split peas and cook for 1 further hour, adding some water if the stock becomes too thick.

3 Add the onions, leeks, celery, potatoes, thyme, caraway seeds and nutmeg, and cook for 30–40 minutes.

4 Remove the ham bone. Cut away the meat, shred it and set aside.

5 Transfer half the pea mixture to a food processor and purée until smooth, then return it to the pan and season with salt, pepper and lemon juice. Add the shredded ham to the soup and reheat gently.

6 Serve the soup piping hot, garnished with thyme sprigs.

Serves 6

490 kcals 62 g carbs 10 g fat 39 g protein 102 mg calcium 6 mg iron 800 mcg vitamin B6 450 mcg vitamin B2 450 mg phosphorus 5.5 mg zinc

Oriental beef & rice noodle soup

250 g (8 oz) rice or egg noodles

1.2 litres (2 pints) beef stock (see page 19)

2.5 cm (1 inch) piece of fresh root ginger, smashed

3 garlic cloves, smashed but left whole

4 kaffir lime leaves

3 red chillies, deseeded and finely sliced

1 cinnamon stick

3 tablespoons soy sauce

1 teaspoon sesame oil

½ teaspoon ground ginger

500 g (1 lb) lean sirloin, fillet or rump steak

200 g (7 oz) pak choi, finely chopped

200 g (7 oz) mangetout, finely sliced

25 g (1 oz) Thai basil, finely chopped

basil or chopped coriander, to garnish

Beef is a good source of vitamin B12, which is known as the 'energizing vitamin', and is usually deficient in people suffering from stress and exhaustion. This soup is a good choice if your nerves have been on edge as B12 is essential for the normal function of nervous tissue.

1 Cook the noodles according to the packet instructions. Drain and rinse in cold water, drain again and set aside until needed.

2 Heat the stock in a large saucepan with the ginger root, garlic, lime leaves, red chillies and cinnamon. Bring to the boil and simmer, covered, for 15 minutes then remove from the heat and leave to infuse.

3 Mix the soy sauce, sesame oil and ground ginger in a bowl. Put the beef in and wipe it around, ensuring you mop up all the marinade. Cover the bowl and leave the steak to marinate for 30 minutes.

4 About 10 minutes before you want to eat, remove the ginger, garlic and cinnamon stick from the stock and return it to a gentle simmer.

5 Heat a large nonstick pan and sear the steak on both sides then cook each side for about 2–3 minutes, or according to taste. Remove and leave on a board to rest.

6 Add the pak choi, mangetout, Thai basil and cold noodles to the simmering stock.

7 Quickly cut the steak into thin slices.

8 Pour the soup into deep soup bowls and place the steak slices on the top. Garnish with extra basil or some coriander.

Serves 4

415 kcals 31 g carbs 13 g fat 43 g protein
6.8 mg iron 74 mcg folate 1 mg vitamin B6
7.15 mg zinc 126 mg vitamin C 167 mg calcium

Irish oyster soup

2 potatoes, diced

1.2 litres (2 pints) chicken stock (see page 19)

125 g (4 oz) lean bacon lardons

25 g (1 oz) parsley, finely chopped

juice of ½ lemon

24 oysters, shucked with juices reserved

salt and pepper

To garnish:

parsley sprigs

finely chopped spring onions

Tabasco sauce (optional)

This fortifying soup is a wonderful booster; oysters are one of the most nutritionally well balanced of foods, containing protein, carbohydrates and lipids. In fact, the National Heart and Lung Institute recommends them for low-cholesterol diets. They are an excellent source of vitamins A, B1 (thiamin), B2 (riboflavin), B3 (niacin), C (ascorbic acid), and D (calciferol). Four or five medium oysters supply the recommended daily allowance of iron, copper, iodine, magnesium, calcium, zinc, manganese and phosphorus. They are also believed to have aphrodisiac qualities – they certainly give low fertility and low sperm counts a boost because of their high zinc and iron content.

1 Put the potatoes and stock into a large saucepan and bring to the boil, then turn down the heat and simmer until the potatoes are done.
2 Meanwhile, cook the lardons in a frying pan over a medium heat until evenly browned.
3 Remove the potato mixture from the heat and let cool. Blend in a food processor until smooth.
4 Pour the soup back into the pan and add the bacon lardons, parsley and lemon juice. Season to taste with salt and pepper and bring back to the boil. Add the oysters and their juice, simmer for a few minutes then serve in warm bowls, garnished with extra parsley, spring onions and a drizzle of Tabasco, if you like.

Serves 4

200 kcals **20 g** carbs **6.7 g** fat **18 g** protein **160 mg** calcium **60 mg** zinc **7 mg** iron **65 mcg** iodine **49 mcg** folate **1 mg** vitamin E **25 mg** vitamin C

resouperation

When you've been through a period of ill health it is vital that you build yourself up again by eating foods that are easily digested and full of nutrients that will aid repair, rebuild wasted tissue and bones, fortify the blood and restore a weakened system. These soups are ideal because they are nutrient rich and easy to digest.

(Left: Spicy Indian broth, see page 87 for recipe.)

Avgolemono

1.8 litres (3 pints) chicken stock (see page 19)

150 g (5 oz) cooked risotto rice or 125 g (4 oz) orzo pasta

3 eggs

juice of 1 large lemon

1 tablespoon cold water

salt and pepper

lemon slices, to garnish

The name *avgolemono* means egg and lemon and this simple Greek spin on chicken soup is light and very nourishing. Its delicate taste makes it easy on stomachs that have been upset and the lemon has natural antiseptic properties that will cleanse the digestive system.

1 Pour the stock into a large saucepan and add the pasta or cooked rice. Bring to the boil and cook for 5 minutes or until the pasta is done.

2 Beat the eggs in a bowl until frothy, then add the lemon juice and cold water. Slowly stir a ladleful of the hot chicken stock into the egg mixture, then add 1 or 2 more. Return this mixture to the pan, take it off the heat and season with salt and pepper. Do not let the soup boil or the eggs will curdle.

3 Serve the soup at once, garnished with lemon slices.

Serves 4–6

206 kcals **21 g** carbs **9 g** fat **13 g** protein **50 mg** calcium

Fruitcake soup

6 slices of dark
pumpernickel bread,
crusts removed

1.2 litres (2 pints) apple
juice

200 ml (7 fl oz) prune juice

75 g (3 oz) clear honey

75 g (3 oz) dried apricots,
roughly chopped

2 Granny Smith apples,
peeled, quartered, cored
and sliced

125 g (4 oz) stoned dried
prunes, chopped

50 g (2 oz) cranberries

1 cinnamon stick and 4
cloves, tied together in a
piece of muslin

grated rind of 1 lemon

To garnish:

4 tablespoons Greek yogurt

sliced fresh fig

mint leaves

clear honey

You might look twice at this soup, but it is an adaptation of an old Estonian recipe – my only regret was saying goodbye to the apple brandy. It is a healthy, sweet treat that makes a nutritious way to end a meal. If you like Christmas pudding, or fruitcake, you will love it. It is very high in carbohydrates, but if you want a sugar hit, then make sure you eat healthy sugars. This is a rich soup, so a little goes a long way. If you are anaemic, it will be very good for you, as it is high in iron and folate.

1 Toast the bread on both sides.
2 Bring the apple juice and prune juice to the boil in a large saucepan, stir in the honey and boil vigorously for 1 minute. Add the bread, reduce the heat to low and simmer until the bread just begins to disintegrate. Remove the bread from the soup, rub it through a sieve, then return it to the pan.
3 Stir in the apricots, apples, prunes, cranberries, cinnamon and cloves and the lemon rind. Bring to the boil, then reduce the heat, cover the pan and simmer for about 15 minutes, or until the fruit is tender.
4 Remove the soup from the heat. Let it cool then chill in the refrigerator for 1–2 hours until you are ready to serve.
5 To serve, ladle the soup into bowls and top with a generous spoonful of Greek yogurt, a couple of fig slices, mint leaves and a drizzle of honey.

Serves 6

287 kcals 67 g carbs 1.7 g fat 4.7 g protein 2.5 mg iron 20 mcg folate 30 mg vitamin C

Thai chicken soup

When you have been ill and lost your appetite, this tasty soup will get your taste buds working again. It will help you to recover from a variety of ailments as the chicken has antiviral properties, the lime is antiseptic and the ginger alleviates nausea and stimulates the digestive system and circulation.

1 Cut the galangal or ginger into thin slices. Split the lemon grass stalks lengthways into two and put them into a saucepan with the coconut milk, chicken stock and lime leaves. Bring to the boil, then reduce the heat and simmer over a low heat for 30 minutes, stirring occasionally.
2 Add the chicken and chilli to the pan and simmer for 8 minutes. Add the fish sauce and sugar and stir to combine.
3 Pour the soup into warm bowls, stir in the coriander and basil leaves and serve immediately, with half a lime on the side.

Serves 4

5 cm (2 inch) piece of fresh galangal or root ginger, peeled

2 lemon grass stalks

500 ml (17 fl oz) coconut milk

250 ml (8 fl oz) chicken stock (see page 19)

10 kaffir lime leaves

625 g (1¼ lb) chicken breast fillets, cut into thin strips

1–2 teaspoons finely chopped red chilli

2 tablespoons Thai fish sauce

1 teaspoon soft brown sugar

handful of coriander leaves

handful of basil leaves

2 limes, halved

205 kcals **10.5 g** carbs **34 g** protein **3.5 g** fat **80 mg** magnesium **4 mg** vitamin C
48 mg calcium **2 mg** zinc

Tofu & papaya soup

This fragrant soup is a satisfying meal in a bowl, with a host of health benefits, and can be served hot or cold. Papaya contains an enzyme called papain that aids digestion since it breaks down protein, while tofu rebalances hormones and lowers LDL (bad cholesterol). This soup is also very high in calcium, which plays a major part in most bodily functions in addition to its primary role of maintaining healthy bones and teeth.

1 Heat the olive oil in a saucepan with the sesame oil and sauté the spring onion, garlic and ginger until soft. Add the chilli and cook for 1 more minute.
2 Add the lemon grass and lime leaves, lime juice and ground coriander. Stir in the stock and papaya and simmer for 15 minutes.
3 Strain the soup through a fine sieve into a clean saucepan. Push it through with a wooden spoon to ensure all the papaya pulp goes through.
4 Add the tofu and cook for 5 minutes then stir in the coconut milk. Serve the soup with a selection of the garnishes.

Serves 4

2 teaspoons olive oil

1 teaspoon sesame oil

1 spring onion, finely chopped

2 garlic cloves, finely chopped

2.5 cm (1 inch) piece fresh root ginger, peeled and finely chopped

1 red chilli, deseeded and finely chopped

1 lemon grass stalk

2 kaffir lime leaves or a strip of lemon rind

juice of 2 limes, or 1 tablespoon lemon juice

2 teaspoons ground coriander

750 ml (1¼ pints) chicken or vegetable stock (see pages 19 and 21)

500 g (1 lb) fresh papaya, peeled, deseeded and diced

250 g (8 oz) silken or firm tofu, diced

2 tablespoons coconut milk

To garnish:

thin strips of red pepper

2 tablespoons roasted peanuts or cashews

2 tablespoons chopped coriander leaves

1 spring onion, finely chopped

205 kcals **17 g** carbs **12 g** fat **8 g** protein **366 mg** calcium **104 mg** vitamin C **195 mcg** vitamin E

Spicy Indian broth

50 g (2 oz) butter

1 large onion, chopped

3 garlic cloves, chopped

1 teaspoon cumin seeds

1 teaspoon ground coriander

pinch of ground cinnamon

pinch of ground nutmeg

1 teaspoon chopped fresh root ginger

½ teaspoon ground cloves

1 red chilli, deseeded and finely chopped

½ teaspoon ground cardamom

200 g (7 oz) dried green lentils

1.2 litres (2 pints) vegetable stock (see page 21)

500 g (1 lb) spinach, finely chopped

250 g (8 oz) Greek yogurt

salt and pepper

handful of coriander leaves, to garnish

The staples of Indian cuisine include foods that are recommended by health professionals to prevent heart disease, obesity, cancer, diabetes and a stroke. Many common dishes are not only nutrient packed, they are also cheap to make. Lentils are little vitamin pills – full of B vitamins – and good for energy production. Dry skin benefits from the vitamin B2 in both the lentils and yogurt, which is also good for digestion. (See page 80 for photograph.)

1 Melt the butter in a large, heavy saucepan, add the onion, garlic, cumin, coriander, cinnamon, nutmeg, ginger, cloves, chilli and cardamom and fry for 5 minutes.
2 Add the lentils and stir for about 2 minutes. Pour in the stock, bring to the boil and simmer, covered, for 1 hour.
3 Add the spinach and simmer for 5 minutes.
4 Stir in the yogurt, season with salt and pepper and heat through gently for 1 minute.
5 Serve the soup in warm bowls, garnished with the coriander leaves.

Serves 6

400 kcals 41 g carbs 19 g fat 22 g protein 335 mg calcium 14 mg iron 220 mcg folate 215 mg magnesium 680 mcg vitamin B2 650 mcg vitamin B6 500 mcg vitamin B1

Chilled roasted garlic & toasted almond soup

1 garlic bulb, skin left on

125 g (4 oz) fresh white breadcrumbs

1 litre (1¾ pints) chicken or vegetable stock (see pages 19 and 21)

125 g (4 oz) blanched almonds, lightly toasted in the oven

5 tablespoons olive oil

1½ tablespoons sherry vinegar

salt and pepper

To garnish:

2 oranges, segmented

halved black and white grapes

toasted almonds

handful of coriander leaves and mint leaves

Almonds will improve your intake of phosphorus and magnesium, which are both crucial minerals for strong bones, so women wanting to reduce the risk or effects of osteoporosis should consider including at least a handful of nuts in their daily diet. Nuts are also known to reduce levels of LDL (bad cholesterol) in the blood. Combined with garlic, which is a powerful blood thinner and general circulatory tonic, this soup is a healthy choice for summertime eating.

1 Roast the garlic bulb in a preheated oven, 180°C (350°F), Gas Mark 4, for about 30 minutes until soft to the touch.
2 Meanwhile, soak the breadcrumbs in 150 ml (¼ pint) of the stock for 5 minutes.
3 Remove the garlic from the oven and let it cool, then squeeze the pulp into the bread mixture.
4 Blend the almonds in a food processor until finely ground. Add the bread mixture to the almonds and blend. Gradually add the oil until it forms a smooth paste, then add the remainder of the stock and the sherry vinegar and process until smooth.
5 Transfer the soup to a bowl and season with salt and pepper. Cover and chill for at least 2–3 hours.
6 Serve the soup in chilled bowls and garnish with the orange segments, grapes, toasted almonds, and coriander and mint.

Serves 6

400 kcals 28 g carbs 28 g fat 10 g protein 125 mg calcium 90 mg magnesium 200 mg phosphorus 8 mg vitamin E

Bouillabaisse

1.5–1.75 kg (3–3½ lb) mixed fish and raw shellfish, such as large prawns, clams, monkfish, red snapper and John Dory

1.2 litres (2 pints) cold water

250 g (8 oz) tomatoes

pinch of saffron threads

2 tablespoons hot water

6 tablespoons olive oil

1 onion, sliced

1 celery stick, sliced

1 leek, sliced

1 bouquet garni

large strip of orange rind

2 garlic cloves, crushed

½ teaspoon fennel seeds

1 tablespoon tomato purée

2 teaspoons Pernod

4 thick slices of French bread

salt and pepper

chervil sprigs, to garnish

This magnificent fish soup, which originated in Marseilles in the south of France, is an excellent meal for anyone recuperating from a long illness. It is packed with healthy protein that will help to rebuild and repair tissues and get you back on your feet again. It is also full of omega-3 fatty acids, so it is a potent brain-boosting broth.

1 Remove the heads, tails and fins from the fish and put the trimmings into a large pan with the water. Bring to the boil and simmer for 20 minutes, then strain and reserve the liquid.

2 Cut the fish into large chunks but leave the shellfish in their shells. Scald the tomatoes in boiling water for 1 minute then immerse in cold water, skin and roughly chop. Soak the saffron in the hot water.

3 Heat the oil in a large saucepan, add the onion, celery and leek and cook gently until softened. Add the bouquet garni, orange rind, garlic, fennel seeds and tomatoes. Stir in the fish stock and the saffron with its soaking liquid and simmer for 30–40 minutes.

4 Add the shellfish and cook for about 6 minutes then add the fish and cook for a further 6–8 minutes, until it flakes easily.

5 Remove the fish and shellfish with a slotted spoon and transfer to a warm serving dish. Rapidly boil the liquid and allow to reduce slightly. Add the tomato purée and Pernod and taste for seasoning.

6 To serve, place a slice of French bread in each bowl and add a selection of fish. Pour over the broth and garnish with chervil.

Serves 4

566 kcals **33 g** carbs **25 g** fat **50 g** protein **170 mg** calcium **3 mg** zinc **3 mg** vitamin E

Chicken, asparagus & tarragon soup

500 g (1 lb) fresh asparagus

2 tablespoons olive oil

125 g (4 oz) celery, sliced

125 g (4 oz) leeks, sliced

125 g (4 oz) onions, sliced

1.2 litres (2 pints) chicken stock (see page 19)

200 g (7 oz) silken tofu

300 g (10 oz) cooked chicken, cut into bite-sized pieces

1 teaspoon chopped thyme

salt and pepper

2 tablespoons chopped tarragon, to garnish

This soup is high in protein, low in carbohydrates and contains only healthy fat. It is an excellent choice for someone following a low carbohydrate diet. If you are recovering from an illness the powerful combination of healthy protein and high calcium will aid your speedy recovery.

1 Trim the bottoms of the asparagus stalks where they begin to turn white. Cut off the tips about 3.5 cm (1½ inches) from the top and set aside. Roughly slice the remaining section.

2 Heat the oil in a large saucepan, add the celery, leeks and onions and fry until soft. Add the stock and bring to the boil. Add the sliced asparagus and simmer for 5 minutes. Remove the soup from the heat and blend in a food processor with the silken tofu.

3 Return the soup to the pan and season with salt and pepper. Add the asparagus tips, the chicken pieces and thyme and simmer for 10 minutes. Pour into warm serving bowls and sprinkle with the chopped tarragon.

Serves 4

270 kcals **32 g** protein **7 g** carbs **12 g** fat **342 mg** calcium **250 mcg** folate **2.5 mg** iron

Leek, apple & potato soup

1.5 litres (2½ pints) chicken or vegetable stock (see pages 19 and 21)

2 large leeks, sliced

500 g (1 lb) sharp green apples, peeled, cored and diced

375 g (12 oz) potatoes, diced

generous pinch of cinnamon

1 teaspoon ground ginger

salt and pepper

Apple dice:

15 g (½ oz) butter

2 apples, peeled, cored and diced

In this recipe, leek and potato soup is given a healthy twist by the addition of sharp green apples, which add a lovely fresh flavour and extra nutritional value. Apples, known as a cleansing food, contain fibre, antioxidants and fruit flavonoids. The most important of these flavonoids is quercetin, which has anti-inflammatory as well as anticancer properties. Apples contain vitamin C as well – the green ones more than the red. They can also reduce blood cholesterol levels, counter constipation and diarrhoea, relieve joint problems, and help prevent diseases in general.

1 Put a little stock in a saucepan and sauté the leeks over a medium heat, covered, for 3–4 minutes. Add the apples and cook, uncovered, for about 5 minutes. Pour in the remaining stock, add the potatoes and bring to the boil. Reduce the heat and simmer for 45 minutes.

2 When the apples and potatoes are soft, blend the soup in a food processor until smooth.

3 Return the soup to the saucepan and stir in the cinnamon and ginger. Season to taste with salt and pepper. Cover and chill in the refrigerator if you are going to serve the soup cold.

4 To make the apple dice, melt the butter in a saucepan and sauté the diced apples for 5 minutes, then drain on kitchen paper.

5 When you are ready to serve, ladle the soup into bowls (reheat it first, if you are serving it hot) and top with the apple dice.

Serves 4

155 kcals **28 g** carbs **4 g** fat **3 g** protein **26 mg** vitamin C **70 mcg** folate

Fresh broad bean
soup with mint

Broad beans are rich in valuable nutrients. They are a good source of iron, magnesium, potassium, zinc, copper, selenium and many vitamins. Their high carbohydrate and protein content makes this soup an effective energy-boosting meal. It is excellent with crusty wholemeal bread and a chunk of dolcelatte cheese.

2 tablespoons olive oil

1 red onion, finely sliced

1.5 kg (3 lb) fresh peas, podded

2 potatoes, sliced

bunch of mint

2 litres (3½ pints) vegetable or chicken stock (see pages 21 and 19)

3 kg (6 lb) young broad beans, podded

salt and pepper

3 tablespoons chopped mint, to garnish

1 Heat the olive oil in a heavy pan and gently fry the onion until soft.

2 Add the peas and potatoes and cook for 5 minutes, stirring continuously. Add half the mint leaves and enough stock to cover. Simmer for 5 minutes then add half the broad beans and simmer for 10 minutes.

3 Put the remaining stock in a separate pan and bring to the boil. Add the remaining beans and the stalks from the bunch of mint. Cook for 3 minutes then drain. Discard the stalks.

4 Put a ladle of the soup mixture into a food processor with a ladle of blanched beans and chop roughly. Set aside.

5 Put the rest of the soup in the food processor with the remaining mint and chop roughly then return to the pan with the remaining broad beans and the puréed bean mixture.

6 Season well with salt and pepper and reheat gently. Serve garnished with the chopped mint.

Serves 6

544 kcals **44 g** protein **11 g** fat **70 g** carbs
230 mg vitamin C **200 mg** magnesium **10 mg** iron
180 mg calcium **6.5 mg** zinc

Borscht

Russian women used to use beetroot juice as rouge, to attract men, but its nutritional benefits far outweigh its aesthetic qualities, as anyone who has stained their hands with beetroot juice will tell you. Beetroot contains phosphorus, sodium, magnesium, calcium, iron and potassium, as well as fibre, vitamins A and C, niacin, folic acid and biotin. It is thought to help fortify the blood, strengthen the liver and bile duct, have tumour-inhibiting powers and to contain betaine, which helps prevent coronary disease.

1 Put the onion, garlic, beetroot, apple, celery, red pepper and mushrooms into a large saucepan with the oil and 3 tablespoons of the stock. Cover and cook gently for 15 minutes, stirring occasionally.

2 Add the cumin seeds and cook for 1 minute, then add the remaining stock, thyme, bay leaf, balsamic vinegar and salt and pepper to taste. Bring to the boil then reduce the heat and simmer for 30 minutes.

3 Let the soup cool then blend in a food processor until smooth and creamy. Return to the pan and reheat.

4 To serve, garnish the soup with swirls of soured cream and some dill sprigs.

Serves 6

1 onion, chopped

2 garlic cloves, chopped

500 g (1 lb) beetroot, peeled and chopped

1 large cooking apple, peeled and chopped

2 celery sticks, chopped

1 red pepper, chopped

125 g (4 oz) mushrooms, chopped

1 tablespoon olive oil

1.8 litres (3 pints) beef stock (see page 19)

1 teaspoon cumin seeds

pinch of dried thyme

1 large bay leaf

2 tablespoons balsamic vinegar

salt and pepper

To garnish:

200 ml (7 fl oz) soured cream

dill sprigs

154 kcals **14 g** carbs **10 g** fat **2.5 mg** iron **145 mcg** folate **40 mg** vitamin C

Duck & plum soup

2 boneless duck breasts, about 400 g (13 oz) each

1 teaspoon Chinese five-spice powder

1.2 litres (2 pints) beef stock (see page 19)

1 tablespoon pomegranate concentrate

250 g (8 oz) chestnut mushrooms, finely sliced

4 Victoria plums, peeled, stoned and quartered

2 spring onions, finely sliced

50 g (2 oz) wild rice, cooked according to packet instructions

salt and pepper

cucumber, cut into julienne strips, to garnish

sesame oil, to drizzle

This soup is full of iron and will provide a valuable dose if you are anaemic, or experiencing a heavy period. Plums are full of potassium which can also help eliminate menstrual bloating. Pomegranate concentrate is available from Middle Eastern stores.

1 Score the skin of the duck breasts and rub with the five-spice powder. Heat a griddle or frying pan over a high heat and cook the duck breasts, skin-side down, until the skin is brown and crispy.
2 Turn over the duck breasts and reduce the heat to medium. Cook the duck breasts for 5–7 minutes, according to taste. Remove from the heat and keep warm.
3 Put the stock into a saucepan with the pomegranate concentrate and boil rapidly until the stock has reduced by about one-quarter.
4 Reduce the heat to a simmer; add the mushrooms, plums, spring onions and wild rice to the pan and cook for 2–3 minutes. Season to taste.
5 Slice the duck breasts and divide among 4 bowls. Remove the onions, mushrooms and plums from the soup with a slotted spoon and arrange around the duck. Pour over the stock. Garnish with the cucumber and drizzle a few drops of sesame oil to taste. Serve immediately.

Serves 4

315 kcals 12 g carbs 23 g fat 18 g protein 3 mg iron

winter warmers

When the temperature drops and we have to spend time in overheated and poorly ventilated buildings where germs spread very easily, our mucous membranes dry out, leaving us more vulnerable to infection, and our bodies use extra energy trying to keep us warm when we are out in the elements. At this time, it is essential that we take in the proper fuel to compensate for those extra demands on our systems and prevent germs taking a hold. These warming soups will bolster your immune system and, should you catch a cold or flu, they will help minimize your symptoms and get you quickly on the road to recovery.

(Right: Lemon & leek soup with coriander & lemon salsa, see page 107 for recipe.)

Chicken & barley soup

1 large chicken, weighing
2.5–3 kg (5–6 lb)

3 onions

3 large carrots

3 celery sticks

12 garlic cloves

1 lemon, halved

4 bay leaves

600 ml (1 pint) water

250 g (8 oz) pearl barley

1 organic chicken stock cube

4 tablespoons chopped
parsley

salt and pepper

The minute that I am feeling slightly under the weather, I make a huge pan of this soup. The results are always miraculous – chicken, garlic, onions and lemons all have antiviral and antibacterial properties.

1 Cut the chicken into quarters and put them into a large saucepan with 1 onion, 1 carrot, 1 celery stick, all quartered, the whole garlic cloves, and the lemon and bay leaves. Add water to cover and bring to the boil. Cover with a lid and simmer for about 1–1½ hours until the meat is tender and pulls away from the bone.

2 Remove the chicken with a slotted spoon and place on a large dish to cool. Remove the carrot, celery, onion and garlic cloves and put them into a food processor. (Alternatively, if you want a clear soup, leave the vegetables in the pan with the stock.)

3 Remove the meat from the chicken bones, chop it into bite-sized pieces and reserve. Skim any fat from the surface of the stock. Put the chicken bones back into the saucepan, discarding any skin. Add the measured water and bring to the boil, then reduce the heat and simmer for 1 hour.

4 Strain the stock through a sieve and return the liquid to the pan. (If you are making a thicker soup, take 1 ladleful of stock and add it to the vegetables in the food processor. Blend and stir into the rest of the stock.) Add the pearl barley and cook for 20 minutes or until done.

5 Finely chop the remaining carrots, onions and celery and add to the stock. Crumble in the stock cube for extra flavour and cook for about 15 minutes until the vegetables are tender. Add the chopped chicken and parsley, check for seasoning and serve.

Serves 8

579 kcals 12 g carbs 28 g fat 44 g protein
94 mg calcium 70 mg magnesium
27 mg vitamin C 3.5 mg zinc

Baba ghanoush soup

Aubergines not only block the formation of free radicals, they also reduce cholesterol levels and are a good source of folic acid and potassium. Sesame seeds also help to protect the body from free radicals. They are a key source of magnesium, calcium and phytic acid, which could inhibit cancer, specifically of the colon.

1 Bake the aubergine in a preheated oven, 200°C (400°F), Gas Mark 6, for 15–20 minutes. Let it cool, then cut it in half and scrape out the flesh. Purée the flesh with the tahini, garlic and a little salt.
2 Put the stock into a large saucepan. Bring to the boil, then reduce the heat to a simmer. Stir in the aubergine mixture, partially cover the pan, then simmer for 30 minutes.
3 Remove the pan from heat and press the soup through a sieve.
4 When you are ready to serve, reheat the soup and season to taste. Beat the egg with the lemon juice and stir it through the simmering soup, to form long egg strands. Simmer for another 2–3 minutes, then ladle the soup into bowls and top with handfuls of fresh chopped parsley and toasted pine nuts. Serve with warm pitta bread.

Serves 4

1 large aubergine

65 g (2½ oz) tahini paste

2 garlic cloves, crushed

1.2 litres (2 pints) chicken or vegetable stock
(see pages 19 and 21)

1 egg

juice of 1 lemon

salt and pepper

pitta bread, to serve

To garnish:

25 g (1 oz) chopped parsley

25 g (1 oz) toasted pine nuts

161 kcals **3.7 g** carbs **14 g** fat **5 g** protein **45 mcg** folate **132 mg** calcium **310 mcg** carotene

French onion soup
with goats' cheese croûtons

4 tablespoons olive oil

750 g (1½ lb) onions, thinly sliced

2 garlic cloves, crushed

2 tablespoons apple juice

1.2 litres (2 pints) beef stock (see page 19)

300 ml (10 fl oz) dry white wine

salt and pepper

chives, to garnish

Croûtons:

1 tablespoon olive oil

1–2 garlic cloves, crushed

3 slices 100% rye bread, cut into quarters

250 g (8 oz) goats' cheese

Onions are an excellent tonic and benefit the body in many ways. They have a decongesting effect on the respiratory tract and, as they cleanse the blood, they improve circulation. This classic soup is given a healthy twist with rye bread and goats' cheese, but if you prefer a more traditional approach, just substitute with the usual slices of French baguette and sticky Gruyère cheese.

1 Heat the oil in a heavy saucepan, add the onions, garlic and apple juice and cook over a high heat for 5–6 minutes, stirring constantly, then turn down the heat to very low and leave the onions to cook for about 20 minutes. The bottom of the pan will turn a deep caramel brown.

2 Pour the stock and the white wine into the onion mixture and season with salt and pepper. Stir with a wooden spoon, scraping all the juices from the bottom and sides of the pan. Bring to a simmer and leave to cook, uncovered, for about 1 hour.

3 Meanwhile, make the croûtons. Drizzle the olive oil on a baking tray, add the crushed garlic and spread evenly. Place the bread in the oil, turning to ensure that both sides are coated. Bake in a preheated oven, 180°F (350°C), Gas Mark 4, for 15 minutes until crispy and crunchy.

4 Spread the croûtons with a thick layer of goats' cheese and sprinkle with pepper. Heat the grill to high, pour the soup into heatproof bowls and put 2 croûtons into each bowl. Place under the grill until the cheese is bubbling. Sprinkle with chives and serve immediately.

Serves 6

365 kcals **31 g** carbs **20 g** fat **13 g** protein **155 mg** calcium **200 mg** phosphorus

Crab, asparagus & sweetcorn soup

1.2 litres (2 pints) chicken stock (see page 19)

2.5 cm (1 inch) piece of fresh root ginger, peeled and smashed

1 teaspoon groundnut oil

175 g (6 oz) cooked white crabmeat

300 g (10 oz) fresh asparagus, finely sliced, with tips left intact

200 g (7 oz) frozen sweetcorn kernels or baby corn, finely sliced

1 tablespoon cornflour, dissolved into 2 tablespoons cold water

1 egg white, lightly beaten

salt and pepper

To garnish:

1 spring onion, finely sliced

2 tablespoons chopped coriander leaves

Sweetcorn is a good source of folate. It also helps protect against age-related macular degeneration and helps fight free radicals in the retina. It is high in iron and potassium and provides more starch and more calories than most vegetables. It is also a good food for steadying blood sugar. It is thought that asparagus stimulates immunity and may also help to lower cholesterol. It is a good source of folate and vitamin E and also contains fructo-oligosaccharides (FOS) which promote the growth of beneficial bacteria in the colon. Asparagus is also a natural diuretic.

1 Put the stock into a large saucepan with the ginger. Bring to the boil and simmer, covered, for 30 minutes.
2 Heat the groundnut oil in another large pan, add the crabmeat with a little salt and pepper and cook for 1 minute.
3 Remove the ginger from the stock with a slotted spoon and pour the stock over the crab mixture. Bring to the boil and add the asparagus. Reduce the heat and simmer for 3 minutes; add the sweetcorn and cook for 2 minutes.
4 Pour in the cornflour mixture and cook for 2 minutes, stirring continuously until the soup has thickened.
5 Take the soup from the heat and, just before serving, pour in the egg whites and stir very slowly, so the egg forms ribbons.
6 Serve the soup in warm deep soup bowls, garnished with the spring onion and coriander.

Serves 4

135 kcals 14 g carbs 3.5 g fat 13 g protein
3.3 mcg zinc 155 mcg folate 1.5 mg vitamin E

Lemon & leek soup with coriander & lemon salsa

15 g (½ oz) butter

4 leeks, cut into 1 cm (½ inch) slices

750 ml (1¼ pints) vegetable stock (see page 21)

1 large egg, lightly beaten

juice of 2 large lemons

pinch of ground cinnamon

salt and pepper

Coriander & lemon salsa:

2 Cos lettuce leaves, thinly sliced

2 garlic cloves, chopped

½ red or green chilli, deseeded and finely chopped

2 tablespoons lemon juice

2 tablespoons olive oil

50 g (2 oz) coriander leaves, roughly chopped

ground cumin

chilli powder

salt and pepper

This sharp and refreshing soup is based on leeks, which have been used in herbal remedies since Roman times. The Romans used them to treat anything from sore throats to kidney stones. They are effective in stimulating the kidneys as they have a diuretic action and combat fluid retention due to their potassium content. They are also high in folate, which is essential for physical and mental health. (See page 100 for photograph.)

1 First make the salsa. Purée the lettuce, garlic, chilli, lemon juice and oil in a food processor. Add the coriander leaves and blend until it becomes a smooth sauce. Season with cumin and chilli powder to taste and salt and pepper. Set aside.

2 Melt the butter over a medium heat and, when it is just foaming, add the leeks and cook for about 10 minutes until soft.

3 Pour in the stock and cook over a medium heat for another 10 minutes. Using a slotted spoon, remove about a quarter of the leeks and put them into a food processor with a little of the hot stock. Blend until smooth then return to the pan.

4 Beat together the egg and lemon juice then add a little of the hot soup mixture, stirring continuously to prevent scrambling. When the mixture is well combined, add another couple of ladlefuls of soup and stir. Pour this mixture back into the soup and heat gently, stirring all the time, until the mixture has thickened slightly. Remove from the heat and add salt, pepper and a pinch of cinnamon.

5 To serve, pour into warm serving bowls and decorate with a swirl of coriander and lemon salsa.

Serves 4

210 kcals **11.5 g** carbs **15 g** fat **7 g** protein **126 mg** calcium **50 mg** vitamin C **20 mcg** folate **2.7 mg** iron

Japanese
chicken soup

1 large potato, cut into small chunks

1 daikon or mooli, peeled, shaved lengthways and cut into thin strips

2 onions, finely sliced

750 g (1½ lb) mixed chicken meat (breasts and thigh fillets), cut into bite-sized chunks

500 g (1 lb) firm tofu, cut into bite-sized cubes

200 g (7 oz) shiitake mushrooms, sliced

1 Savoy cabbage, shredded

300 g (10 oz) baby corn, cut into 1 cm (½ inch) chunks

150 ml (¼ pint) soy sauce

1.2 litres (2 pints) chicken stock (see page 19)

125 ml (4 fl oz) mirin, dry sherry or sake

salt and pepper

This stew is traditionally the fare of Sumo wrestlers, despite it being incredibly healthy and low in fat. The chicken and tofu supply high-quality protein and a generous dose of calcium, while the cabbage gives it powerful antioxidant and digestive tract-cleansing properties. It is very light and easy to digest – a perfect chicken soup. The daikon or mooli is a giant white radish available from Oriental and Asian stores.

1 Parboil the potato and daikon strips in boiling water for 10 minutes then drain and reserve.
2 Put the onions, chicken, tofu, mushrooms, cabbage and corn into a large pan with the soy sauce.
3 Bring the chicken stock to the boil in another pan and add to the chicken mixture. Stir and simmer for about 10 minutes until the chicken is cooked.
4 Add the potato, daikon and mirin, season with salt and pepper and cook for a few more minutes. Serve steaming hot.

Serves 6

400 kcals 37 g carbs 7 g fat 42 g protein 260 mcg folate 400 mcg phosphorus
1 mg vitamin B6 90 mg vitamin C

Celery & horseradish soup

400 g (13 oz) celery, roughly chopped

1 onion, roughly chopped

4 garlic cloves, crushed

1.2 litres (2 pints) chicken stock (see page 19)

2 teaspoons fresh grated horseradish

1 tablespoon white wine vinegar

salt and pepper

chopped parsley, to garnish

This heart-warming combination will set you on the road to recovery if you have a cold. Horseradish, along with onions and garlic, helps to break down mucus, and celery will replenish your diminishing potassium reserves and has a marvellous anti-inflammatory effect. In addition, you have the extra antibacterial and antiviral properties of chicken stock.

1 Put the celery, onion, garlic and stock into a large saucepan. Bring to the boil then reduce the heat, cover and simmer for 30 minutes.
2 Take the pan off the heat, let it cool slightly, then blend the soup in a food processor until smooth.
3 Return the soup to the pan, season with salt and pepper and reheat gently.
4 Add the horseradish and vinegar, stir and serve sprinkled with chopped parsley.

Serves 4

30 kcals **4.8 g** carbs **1.7 g** protein **80 mg** potassium **20 mg** vitamin C **200 mcg** vitamin E

Haitian chicken & orange consommé

This simple consommé can be served hot or cold, and makes a perfect beverage when you have a cold, or a light starter at other times. The orange juice provides vitamin C and combines perfectly with the restorative powers of a good chicken stock. If you feel the need for a little extra nutrition, add some julienne strips of carrot, mangetout and ginger, with a little shredded chicken.

1 Put the chicken stock, orange juice, cloves, star anise and peppercorns into a large pan and simmer gently, covered, for 30 minutes.
2 Strain the soup through a sieve and serve in warm bowls garnished with thin orange slices. Alternatively, chill and serve cold.

Serves 6

27 kcals **6.7 g** carbs **0.5 g** protein **40 mg** vitamin C

1.5 litres (2½ pints) chicken stock (see page 19)

500 ml (17 fl oz) freshly squeezed orange juice, strained

2 cloves

2 star anise

1 teaspoon black peppercorns

orange slices, to garnish

111

Chunky veggie
chowder

1 tablespoon olive oil

25 g (1 oz) butter

1 onion, finely chopped

1 leek, finely chopped

1 celery stick, finely chopped

3 garlic cloves, chopped

2 carrots, sliced

250 g (8 oz) squash, peeled and diced

175 g (6 oz) potatoes, peeled and diced

1 litre (1¾ pints) vegetable stock (see page 21)

175 g (6 oz) broccoli florets

125 g (4 oz) frozen sweetcorn kernels

200 g (7 oz) canned tomatoes

150 ml (5 fl oz) soya milk

salt and pepper

torn basil leaves, to garnish

Chowders are hearty and filling and, when they are this full of immune-boosting antioxidants, they are a perfect antidote to cold winter weather. If you feel a cold is on the way, add a few extra garlic cloves and sprinkle in a few drops of Echinacea to give your system a boost. Most important, don't overcook the chowder – you need to retain maximum nutritional value.

1 Heat the oil and butter in a large heavy saucepan, add the onion, leek, celery and garlic and cook gently until softened.

2 Add the carrots, squash and potatoes and stir for about 5 minutes. Add the stock, cover and cook for 10 minutes.

3 Add the broccoli, sweetcorn and tomatoes and cook for 5 minutes. Remove from the heat and let cool slightly. Stir in the soya milk and season with salt and pepper to taste.

4 Put the soup into a food processor and blend to a rough purée. You should still be able to see the vibrant colours.

5 Pour the soup back into the pan and gently reheat. Serve in warm bowls, scattered with basil leaves.

Serves 4

240 kcals **29 g** carbs **11.5 g** fat **6.5 g** protein **6.3 mg** betacarotene **467 mcg** vitamin B6 **96 mg** calcium **31 mg** vitamin C

113

detox

Years of abusing your system with toxins, heavy food and drink, irregular eating and sleeping patterns, lack of exercise and high stress levels will lead to a sluggish bloated system, an overall lack of energy and dull skin. Eating fruit for breakfast and one of the soups in this chapter with a mixed salad for lunch and dinner on just a couple of days a week will leave you feeling energized and rejuvenated.

(Left: Cucumber & melon souper cooler, see page 125 for recipe.)

Apple & peanut butter soup

This tasty unusual soup will detoxify your system and leave you feeling energized. The soya milk is full of phytoestrogens so this is a good choice for women approaching the menopause. This soup is also good chilled.

1 Pour the soya milk into a saucepan and heat to just below boiling point.
2 Grate the apple and add it to the milk with the peanut butter, lemon juice, oats and ginger and simmer for 15 minutes.
3 Let the soup cool then blend in a food processor. Pour back into the saucepan and reheat, then taste for seasoning.
4 Serve in warm bowls with a sprinkling of parsley.

Serves 6

1.2 litres (2 pints) soya milk

1 cooking apple

4 tablespoons crunchy peanut butter

juice of 1 lemon

3 tablespoons porridge oats

¼ teaspoon ground ginger

salt and pepper

chopped parsley, to garnish

180 kcals **27 g** carbs **6 g** fat **6 g** protein **20 mg** calcium **30 mg** magnesium

Tofu miso soup

Miso is a soya bean paste that has been a mainstay of Japanese cooking for hundreds of years, and, as it contains powerful isoflavones such as genistein, it has been attributed with anticancer properties particularly in cases of breast and prostate cancer. Soy-rich foods are also believed to reduce LDL (bad cholesterol).

250 g (8 oz) firm tofu

1 spring onion

1 litre (1¾ pints) water

75 g (3 oz) dashi granules

100 g (3½ oz) miso

1 tablespoon mirin or dry sherry

1 sheet toasted nori seaweed, crumbled into small pieces

1 Cut the tofu into 1 cm (½ inch) cubes. Slice the spring onion diagonally into 1 cm (½ inch) lengths.

2 Using a wooden spoon, combine the water and dashi granules in a small saucepan, then bring the mixture to the boil. Reduce the heat to medium, add the miso and mirin and stir to combine, taking care the mixture does not boil as overheating will result in the loss of miso flavour.

3 Add the tofu cubes to the hot stock and heat without boiling over a medium heat for 5 minutes. Serve in warm bowls sprinkled with the spring onion and nori.

Serves 4

105 kcals **6.4 g** carbs **4.2 g** fat **8 g** protein
370 mg calcium **1.8 mg** zinc

Spring vegetable
broth with pesto

1.5 litres (2½ pints) vegetable stock (see page 21)

4 tablespoons extra virgin olive oil

2 garlic cloves, finely sliced

8 spring onions, finely sliced

1 fennel bulb, finely chopped

100 g (3½ oz) fresh asparagus, finely sliced, with tips left intact

1 large cauliflower, divided into small florets

2 large courgettes, sliced

6 tomatoes, skinned, deseeded and finely chopped

200 g (7 oz) green beans, finely sliced

100 g (3½ oz) peas

100 g (3½ oz) broad beans

salt and pepper

small handful of basil, to garnish

Pesto:

75 g (3 oz) basil leaves

50 g (2 oz) pine nuts

3 garlic cloves

50 g (2 oz) Parmesan cheese, roughly grated

4 tablespoons olive oil

This fusion of fresh vegetables, lightly cooked and full of flavour, is a detoxer's delight. If you want a little more substance, add a little cooked brown rice or wholemeal pasta to each bowl before serving. The fresher the vegetables, the higher the phytonutrient content, so pack the soup with organic produce and feel your body saying thank you.

1 First make the pesto. Put the basil, pine nuts, garlic and Parmesan in a food processor and blend. With the machine running, slowly add the olive oil through the funnel. Transfer to a small bowl and set aside.

2 Bring the stock to the boil in a large saucepan. Heat the olive oil in a flameproof casserole over a medium heat, add the garlic, spring onions and fennel and cook gently without colouring for about 10 minutes.

3 Add the asparagus, cauliflower, courgettes, tomatoes, green beans, peas and broad beans, pour in the boiling stock and simmer for 10 minutes.

4 Season with salt and pepper and serve in large bowls with a tablespoon of pesto in the middle and sprinkled with basil.

Serves 4

375 kcals 18 g carbs 27 g fat 15 g protein 240 mg calcium 6 mg iron 86 mg magnesium 142 mg vitamin C 2.5 mg zinc

Spinach & rice soup

750 g (1½ lb) spinach, finely chopped

1.2 litres (2 pints) chicken or vegetable stock (see pages 19 and 21)

3 tablespoons olive oil

1 onion, finely chopped

2 garlic cloves, finely chopped

1 small red chilli, deseeded and finely chopped

125 g (4 oz) risotto rice

salt and pepper

4 tablespoons finely grated Parmesan or Pecorino cheese, to serve

The key to a good detox is choosing simple ingredients that won't overtax your system. The spinach is rich in vitamin C and the rice full of B vitamins. This soup will sustain rather than drain you and keep your energy levels up and your mood high.

1 Place the spinach in a saucepan with 2 tablespoons of the stock and heat until wilted. Set aside.

2 Heat the oil in a large saucepan, add the onion, garlic and chilli and cook for 3–4 minutes, until softened.

3 Stir in the rice until well coated with the oil. Pour in the stock and bring to the boil then reduce the heat and simmer for 10 minutes.

4 Add the spinach and any liquid, season with salt and pepper and cook for 5–7 minutes until the rice is done.

5 Serve the soup in warm bowls, sprinkled with the grated Parmesan or Pecorino.

Serves 4

365 kcals **35 g** carbs **18 g** fat **16 g** protein **7 mg** iron **240 mcg** folate **100 mg** vitamin C **180 mg** magnesium **380 mg** calcium

Artichoke bisque

6 large fresh or frozen artichoke hearts, about 500 g (1 lb) in total

25 g (1 oz) butter

1 tablespoon olive oil

3 garlic cloves

900 ml (1½ pints) vegetable or chicken stock
(see pages 21 and 19)

1 baking potato, diced

salt and pepper

8 small mushrooms, finely sliced, to garnish

Artichokes are a valuable source of vitamins A and C, and good for the digestive tract. As they are from the thistle family, they are particularly effective at detoxifying an overworked liver. This soup has a lovely nutty flavour and is naturally thickened by the potato, instead of the usual white flour.

1 Thinly slice the artichoke hearts. Melt the butter with the oil in a frying pan, add the garlic and sliced artichokes and sauté gently until the artichokes are tender. Using a slotted spoon, transfer the mixture to a large saucepan, setting the oily pan aside.

2 Add the stock and potato to the artichoke mixture and bring to the boil. Cover and simmer for about 10–15 minutes, until the artichokes and potatoes are cooked.

3 Meanwhile, put the mushrooms in the oiled pan and fry over a medium heat, tossing frequently, until they are browned and slightly crispy at the edges.

4 Remove the soup from the heat and purée in a food processor until smooth. Season to taste. Transfer to warm bowls and garnish with the mushroom slices.

Serves 4

280 kcals **33 g** carbs **10 g** fat **10 g** protein **155 mg** calcium

Mangetout, mint & caviar soup

1 large Spanish onion, chopped

2 garlic cloves, roughly chopped

250 g (8 oz) leek, roughly chopped

1.5 litres (2½ pints) chicken or vegetable stock (see pages 19 and 21)

125 g (4 oz) dried butter beans, soaked overnight, or 250 g (8 oz) canned butter beans

1 thyme sprig

1 bay leaf

250 g (8 oz) mangetout or sugar snap peas

bunch of mint, leaves removed from the stalks

salt and pepper

To garnish:

1 tablespoon fromage frais

2 tablespoons caviar or fish roe, black or red

Peas and beans are very high in fibre and will act as an intestinal brush, clearing out impacted toxins and waste matter. The onion, leek and garlic will help purify the blood and vital organs.

1 Sweat the onion, garlic and leek with a little stock, covered, in a flameproof casserole until softened.
2 Add the butter beans, stock and herbs and boil for 10 minutes, then transfer the casserole to a preheated oven, 180°C (350°F), Gas Mark 4. Cover and cook for 40 minutes (or 20 minutes if using canned beans), or until the beans are done.
3 Remove the casserole from the oven, add the mangetout or sugar snap peas and the mint leaves, reserving a few leaves for garnish, and boil for 5 minutes. Transfer to a food processor and blend until smooth. Pass the soup through a fine sieve, return to the pan and season with salt and pepper to taste.
4 Serve the soup in warm bowls, with a swirl of fromage frais and a dollop of caviar or fish roe. Finish with a mint leaf and serve immediately.

Serves 4

175 kcals 29 g carbs 1.5 g fat 12.5 g protein 163 mg calcium 56 mg vitamin C
1.5 mg zinc 2 mg vitamin E 400 mcg vitamin B6 450 mcg vitamin B5
6 mg iron 86 mg magnesium 650 mcg carotene

123

Raw energy
soup with alfalfa sprouts

This raw twist on a classic borscht recipe is a high-energy soup which pumps your body full of detoxifying and immune-boosting nutrients. Alfalfa sprouts contain abundant food enzymes that are attributed with anti-ageing powers – a biogenic food source.

1 Put the beetroot, carrot, cucumber, red pepper, tomatoes and lemon in a food processor and blend until finely chopped. Add the avocado, spinach, alfalfa sprouts and dill. With the machine running, gradually add the vegetable stock and process until smooth.
2 Transfer the soup to a bowl, cover and refrigerate for at least 2 hours until well chilled. Season to taste and serve the soup in chilled bowls, garnished with alfalfa sprouts.

Serves 4

1 large beetroot, peeled and cut into chunks

1 carrot, sliced

1 small cucumber, peeled and cut into chunks

1 red pepper, cored, deseeded and roughly chopped

6 tomatoes, skinned, deseeded and chopped

1 lemon, peeled, halved and deseeded

1 ripe avocado, peeled, stoned and quartered

75 g (3 oz) spinach

75 g (3 oz) alfalfa sprouts, plus extra to garnish

25 g (1 oz) dill, chopped

500 ml (17 fl oz) vegetable stock (see page 21)

salt and pepper

165 kcals **16 g** carbs **8 g** fat **5 g** protein **3 mg** iron **100 mg** vitamin C

Cucumber & melon
souper cooler

400 g (13 oz) Galia melon flesh, deseeded and roughly chopped

1 cucumber, peeled, deseeded and roughly chopped

2 tablespoons finely chopped mint

600 ml (1 pint) dry white grape juice

2 tablespoons Greek yogurt

2 ice cubes (optional)

To garnish:

chopped strawberries

cucumber slices

mint leaves

This is one of the simplest chilled soups and should not take more than 10 minutes to make. It is excellent for a summer detox and can be served as a soup or as a shake in a tall glass. Melons are a good source of betacarotene and vitamin C and they may have an anticoagulant action on the blood. Melons are also thought to reduce the risk of cancer and heart disease. Cucumbers are packed with potassium, so they make good diuretics and help reduce fluid retention. (See page 114 for photograph.)

1 Blend the melon, cucumber, mint, grape juice and yogurt in a food processor for 1 minute. If you are going to serve the soup immediately, add a couple of ice cubes with the ingredients. Alternatively, transfer the soup to a bowl and chill in the refrigerator for at least 2 hours.
2 Serve in bowls, garnished with the strawberries, cucumber slices and mint leaves.

Serves 4

110 kcals **25 g** carbs **2 g** protein **85 mg** calcium **20 mg** vitamin C **300 mg** potassium

Scallop & broccoli broth

1.2 litres (2 pints)
vegetable or chicken stock
(see pages 21 and 19)

25 g (1 oz) fresh root
ginger, peeled and cut into
julienne strips, peel
reserved

1 tablespoon soy sauce

3 spring onions, cut into
fine diagonal slices

500 g (1 lb) broccoli,
trimmed and cut into
small florets

1 small red chilli,
deseeded and finely sliced
(optional)

12 large scallops, with roes

Thai fish sauce, to taste

juice of ½ lime

sesame oil, to serve

This soup will detoxify your mind as well as your body. It is extremely light and an excellent choice for giving an overburdened system a rest. With the addition of rice noodles, it can make an ideal light lunch or supper. Broccoli is a valuable food as it builds health and contains sulphoraphane which helps neutralize cancer-causing substances in the gut. It also helps to lower the risk of a stroke and heart diseases and may reduce the risk of cataracts as well. It is rich in nutrients, helps fight anaemia and lessens the risk of spina bifida. Scallops provide those all-important omega-3 fatty acids. These have been proved to prevent some cancers, to lower the risk of heart disease by preventing blood clots and cholesterol build-up, help cure mental ailments and much more.

1 Put the stock into a large saucepan with the ginger peel and boil for 15 minutes. Set aside and allow to steep for a further 15 minutes.
2 Strain the stock into a clean saucepan. Add the soy sauce, julienne strips of ginger, spring onions, broccoli and chilli, if using, and simmer for 5 minutes.
3 Add the scallops, simmer for a further 3 minutes, or until the scallops are just cooked through. Season with fish sauce and lime juice.
4 Remove the scallops from the soup with a slotted spoon and put 3 in each soup bowl. Divide the broccoli among the bowls and pour in the hot soup. Serve immediately with a few drops of sesame oil.

Serves 4

318 kcals   11 g carbs   4.5 g fat   58 g protein   120 mg vitamin C   6.8 mg zinc
120 mg magnesium   165 mcg folate   146 mg calcium

Fennel & tomato gazpacho

This light, vitamin-packed soup is ideal for a summer detox and boosting the immune system. Fennel is a natural diuretic and is also rich in phytoestrogens. It is good for calming hot flushes.

1 Pour boiling water over the tomatoes and leave for about 1 minute. Drain and skin carefully then chop roughly.

2 Trim the green fronds from the fennel and reserve. Finely slice the bulb and put it into a saucepan with the boiling water and the rock salt. Cover and simmer for 10 minutes.

3 Crush the coriander seeds and peppercorns using a pestle and mortar. Heat the olive oil in a large saucepan and add the crushed spices, garlic and onion. Cook gently for 5 minutes.

4 Add the balsamic vinegar, lemon juice, tomatoes and oregano and stir well. Add the fennel with its cooking liquid and the tomato purée. Bring to a simmer and leave to cook uncovered for 30 minutes.

5 Blend the soup to a purée in a food processor. Let it cool then chill for at least 2 hours.

6 Serve the soup garnished with the reserved fennel fronds.

Serves 4

750 g (1½ lb) ripe red tomatoes

1 large fennel bulb

300 ml (½ pint) boiling water

1 rounded teaspoon rock salt

¾ teaspoon coriander seeds

½ teaspoon mixed peppercorns

1 tablespoon extra virgin olive oil

1 large garlic clove, crushed

1 small onion, chopped

1 tablespoon balsamic vinegar

1 tablespoon lemon juice

¾ teaspoon chopped oregano

1 teaspoon tomato purée

88 kcals **2.5 g** protein **10 g** carbs **4.5 g** fat **40 mg** vitamin C **45 mg** calcium **22 mg** magnesium

weight loss

You should never lose weight at the expense of your health. It is essential to eat fresh food full of nutrients that will support all bodily functions and maintain energy levels. Flavour is important and variety will help you stick to a more controlled way of eating. All the soups in this chapter have fewer calories than a bar of chocolate or a couple of biscuits, and should help you to stick to your healthy regime and do your body the power of good.

(Left: Two pepper duet, see page 135 for recipe.)

Yogurt & cucumber soup

1 large cucumber, peeled

425 g (14 oz) natural live yogurt

2 garlic cloves, crushed

2 tablespoons white wine vinegar or lemon juice

1 tablespoon roughly chopped mint

salt and pepper

mint sprigs, to garnish

pitta bread, to serve

Live yogurt soothes the intestinal tract and replaces beneficial bacteria, while garlic has a strong antibacterial effect. If you have been suffering from a stomach upset, this chilled Middle Eastern soup will get you back on track. It is low in fat and calories, so serve it with a couple of wholemeal pitta breads for a satisfying light meal or snack.

1 Roughly grate the cucumber and place it in a bowl with the yogurt, garlic, vinegar and mint. Season to taste with salt and pepper and chill for at least 2 hours before serving.

2 Pour into individual bowls and garnish with mint sprigs. Serve with warm pitta bread.

Serves 4

80 kcals **9.5 g** carbs **3.5 g** fat **6 g** protein **185 mg** calcium

Celeriac, leek & sage soup

2 large leeks

1 teaspoon extra virgin olive oil

1 large celeriac head, about 400 g (13 oz), peeled and roughly cubed

1 onion, roughly chopped

1 garlic clove, finely chopped

1 litre (1¾ pints) vegetable or chicken stock (see pages 21 and 19)

1 bay leaf

handful of sage

salt and pepper

Celeriac is a good vegetable for weight loss as 112 grams contains only 30 calories. It does not contain cholesterol and provides an excellent source of dietary fibre. Because of its consistency, it adds bulk to dishes as well as flavour and will leave you feeling full.

1 Reserve half of 1 leek and cut the remainder into chunks.
2 Heat the oil in a saucepan and sweat the remaining leeks, celeriac, onion and garlic, covered, until soft.
3 Add the stock, bay leaf and sage and bring to the boil. Cover the pan and simmer for 20 minutes.
4 Cut the reserved leek into fine strips and blanch for 1 minute in salted water.
5 Blend the soup in a food processor until smooth. Season to taste with salt and pepper and serve in warm bowls, garnished with the blanched leek strips.

Serves 4

107 kcals **15 g** carbs **3 g** fat **4.5 g** protein **262 mg** calcium **35 mg** vitamin C

Asparagus & brown rice soup

This soup is a good filler and can be served with a satisfying rough texture, or blended to a smooth consistency if you prefer. Serve with a large green side salad as a lunch or supper dish.

1 Put the stock, celery, onion, carrot, soy sauce and Tabasco sauce into a large saucepan and bring to the boil. Reduce the heat and simmer for 15 minutes.

2 Add the asparagus and the cooked rice and cook for 15 minutes more.

3 To serve, ladle into warm bowls and sprinkle with the chopped spring onions.

Serves 4

1.2 litres (2 pints) chicken or vegetable stock (see pages 19 and 21)

2 celery sticks, chopped

½ onion, chopped

1 carrot, grated

1 tablespoon soy sauce

½ teaspoon Tabasco sauce

250 g (8 oz) fresh asparagus, sliced into 1 cm (½ inch) pieces

150 g (5 oz) brown rice, cooked according to packet instructions

chopped spring onions, to garnish

165 kcals **35 g** carbs **1.5 g** fat **5 g** protein
5 mg carotene **366 mcg** vitamin B1 **140 mcg** folate

Two pepper duet

Red soup:

2 red peppers

400 g (13 oz) can tomatoes

1 garlic clove, crushed

pinch of paprika

¼ teaspoon ground cumin

1 tablespoon lemon juice

salt and pepper

Yellow soup:

3 yellow peppers

1 small potato, cubed

about 500 ml (17 fl oz) chicken stock (see page 19)

½ teaspoon saffron threads, crushed

100 g (3½ oz) Greek yogurt

Despite being a work of art, this soup, or rather soups, is very good for you, as peppers are an excellent source of vitamin C, contain high antioxidant levels and are linked to a reduced risk of heart disease. If you are dieting, the presentation should take your mind off any feelings of denial you may be experiencing. (See page 130 for photograph.)

1 Roast the red and yellow peppers in a preheated oven, 240°C (475°F), Gas Mark 9, for 10–20 minutes, until the skins are blackened. Put them into a plastic bag for 10 minutes, then peel, deseed, core and chop.

2 Combine the red peppers, the tomatoes with their juice, garlic, paprika, cumin and salt and pepper in a saucepan and bring to the boil. Reduce the heat and simmer for 30 minutes.

3 Meanwhile, combine the yellow peppers, potato, stock, crushed saffron and salt and pepper in a second saucepan. Bring to the boil, then reduce the heat and simmer for 30 minutes until the potato is tender.

4 Remove both pans from the heat and let cool slightly.

5 Purée the red pepper mixture in a food processor until very smooth then return it to the pan, stir in the lemon juice and keep warm until you are ready to serve.

6 Purée the yellow pepper mixture in the food processor until very smooth then mix in the yogurt. Add more stock, if necessary, until the soup is approximately the same consistency as the red soup. Return to the pan and keep warm until ready to serve. Alternatively, chill both soups in the refrigerator until very cold.

7 When you are ready to serve, taste both soups for seasoning, Serve in flat soup plates, pouring the two soups simultaneously from opposite sides of the plate until they meet in the middle. Then, with a sharp knife point, slice the red soup a few times into the yellow soup, to make an abstract design.

Serves 4

146 kcals **24 g** carbs **3.3 g** fat **6.6 g** protein **350 mg** vitamin C **3.3 mg** vitamin E **2.5 mg** iron

Summer soup

750 g (1½ lb) ripe
nectarines

250 ml (8 fl oz) freshly
squeezed grapefruit juice

125 ml (4 fl oz) white
grape juice or dry white
wine

¼ teaspoon Tabasco sauce

1 tablespoon balsamic
vinegar

2 tablespoons chopped
coriander leaves

salt and pepper

Nectarines are low in calories and one large nectarine provides almost three-quarters of the daily vitamin C requirement. The fruit has a gentle laxative effect and is also rich in iron and potassium.

1 Purée the nectarines in a food processor with the grapefruit juice, grape juice or wine, Tabasco and balsamic vinegar. Add salt and pepper to taste.
2 Add the coriander and chop roughly, then cover and chill. Serve the soup in small bowls or cups.

Serves 4

104 kcals **23 g** carbs **2.7 g** protein **85 mg** vitamin C **1.5 mg** iron

Creamy fennel & orange soup

1.2 litres (2 pints) chicken or vegetable stock (see pages 19 and 21)

large piece of orange rind, pith removed

3 garlic cloves, finely chopped

1 onion, finely chopped

400 g (13 oz) fennel bulbs, finely sliced

150 g (5 oz) silken tofu

salt and pepper

To garnish:

fennel fronds

orange rind curls

Fennel is a traditional aid to digestion. It can ease stomach cramps and may help to regulate hormone levels. It is also used to treat coughs, can help to counter high blood pressure and is a natural diuretic. This light, low-calorie soup can be drunk regularly throughout the day to stave off hunger pangs.

1 Put the stock and the orange rind into a saucepan and simmer, covered, for 30 minutes.
2 Add the garlic, onion and fennel and simmer, covered, for 30–45 minutes.
3 Remove the orange rind and purée the soup in a food processor. If you want a really smooth soup, strain it through a fine sieve. Add the tofu and blend again until smooth. Return the soup to the pan, season with salt and pepper and reheat.
4 To serve, garnish with fennel fronds and orange rind curls.

Serves 4

60 kcals **6.2 g** carbs **1.9 g** fat **4.8 g** protein **1 mg** iron **225 mg** calcium

Courgette & yellow pepper soup

The yellow pepper in this recipe is packed with cancer-fighting phytochemicals; it also helps kill harmful bacteria in the body and acts as a digestive aid. Peppers stimulate protective mucous membranes in the stomach to ease intestinal inflammation and relieve pain caused by ulcers. They can also buffer pain from other ailments including arthritis, headaches, menstrual cramps and varicose veins, as well as respiratory conditions such as asthma.

2 large yellow courgettes, sliced

1 yellow pepper, cored, deseeded and chopped

2 garlic cloves, crushed

1 tablespoon chopped thyme leaves

1 litre (1¾ pints) chicken stock (see page 19)

4 tablespoons low-fat cream cheese

salt and pepper

thyme sprigs, to garnish

1 Put the courgettes, pepper, garlic and thyme into a saucepan with the chicken stock and simmer for 10 minutes.

2 Blend the soup in a food processor, solids first, until smooth. Add the cream cheese and blend until the cheese has melted into the soup. Season with salt and pepper.

3 Return the soup to the pan and reheat gently.

4 Serve in warm bowls, garnished with thyme sprigs. This soup is also good chilled.

Serves 4

108 kcals **8 g** carbs **7.5 g** fat **2.7 g** protein
65 mg vitamin C **480 mcg** carotene

Cabbage soup

Cabbage soup is a healthy and effective way to help you lose weight, as well as making a nutritious detoxifying soup that is excellent for cleansing the colon and ridding the body of toxins. Be aware that this diet approach should only be undertaken under medical supervision, and is certainly no substitute for a healthy balanced diet. I have adapted the basic recipe and given two extra variations. Try varying the texture and the seasonings to keep the inevitable feelings of monotony at bay. The method is the same for all three variations.

Variation 1

1 Savoy cabbage

2 large onions

4 garlic cloves

875 g (1¾ lb) canned chopped tomatoes

2 green peppers

2 celery sticks

6 carrots

250 g (8 oz) green beans, sliced

2–3 tablespoons vegetable bouillon powder

oregano and thyme

pepper

vegetable stock (see page 21), **to achieve the desired consistency**

Variation 2

1 red cabbage

2 large red onions

4 garlic cloves

875 g (1¾ lb) canned chopped tomatoes

5 red peppers

5 carrots

tarragon and basil

100 ml (3½ fl oz) balsamic vinegar

pepper

vegetable stock (see page 21), **to achieve the desired consistency**

Variation 3

1 white cabbage

2 large onions

4 garlic cloves

2 large fennel bulbs

4 yellow peppers

4 celery sticks

250 g (8 oz) asparagus

2 litres (3½ pints) vegetable stock (see page 21)

½ teaspoon ground cumin

½ teaspoon ground coriander

½ teaspoon ground turmeric

coriander leaves

1 With all the above variations, put all the ingredients into a large pan. Bring to the boil and reduce to a simmer until the vegetables are soft.

2 Season to taste and serve hot or cold.

Each batch makes about 10 small servings

83 kcals **13 g** carbs **10 mg** carotene **96 mg** vitamin C **2.3 mg** iron **170 mcg** folate

78 kcals **15 g** carbs **10 mg** carotene **143 mg** vitamin C **1.4 mg** iron **66 mcg** folate

60 kcals **9 g** carbs **213 mcg** carotene **100 mg** vitamin C **107 mg** iron **96 mcg** folate

Basic principles of the Cabbage Soup diet

Eat as much of the soup as you like, and as often as you like. In addition, you can eat as much as you like on any given day from the list below, unless otherwise specified.

DAY 1: All fruits except bananas.

DAY 2: All vegetables, raw or cooked. This includes a baked potato with a *little* butter.

DAY 3: Fruits and vegetables, but no potatoes or bananas.

DAY 4: Bananas and skimmed milk – eat as many as 8 bananas and drink as many as 8 glasses of skimmed milk.

DAY 5: Beef, skinless chicken and/or fish – as much as 625 g (1¼ lb) in all. You can also eat 6 tomatoes. And you must drink 8 glasses of water. Don't forget at least one bowl of soup.

DAY 6: Beef, skinless chicken, or fish and vegetables. Drink 8 glasses of water and eat at least one bowl of soup.

DAY 7: Brown rice, vegetables (except potatoes) and unsweetened fruit juice.

Index

Acknowledgements

Executive editor Nicky Hill
Project editor Alice Tyler

Executive art editor Geoff Fennell
Designer Adrian Morris

Production controller Manjit Sihra

Photographer Stephen Conroy / © Octopus Publishing Group Ltd
Home Economist David Morgan
Stylist Angela Swaffield